S T U D E N T - F R I E N D L Y   G U I D E S

THE UNIVERSITY OF
WINCHESTI

Excellent dissertations!

STUDENT-FRIENDLY GUIDES

Excellent dissertations !

PETER LEVIN

Open University Press

Open University Press
McGraw-Hill Education
McGraw-Hill House
Shoppenhangers Road
Maidenhead
Berkshire
England
SL6 2QL

email: enquiries@openup.co.uk
world wide web: www.openup.co.uk

and Two Penn Plaza, New York, NY 10121-2289, USA

First published 2005
Reprinted 2005 (twice), 2006 (twice)
Reprinted 2007 (twice), 2008, 2009

A catalogue record of this book is available from the British Library

ISBN 13 978 0035 21822 6 (pb)
ISBN 10 0335 21822 9 (pb)

Library of Congress Cataloging-in-Publication Data
CIP data applied for

Typeset by YHT Ltd, London
Printed in the UK by Bell & Bain Ltd, Glasgow

Mixed Sources
Product group from well-managed
forests and other controlled sources
www.fsc.org Cert no. TT-COC-002769
© 1996 Forest Stewardship Council

FSC

Contents

List of Tables   vii

List of Boxes   viii

Producing a dissertation. READ THIS FIRST!   1

Introduction   5

Part One: Preliminaries
Formal requirements and arrangements   9

Pleasing the examiners   14

You and your supervisor   17

Part Two: Getting started
The 'twin-track': Your project and your dissertation   23

Project and dissertation: Exploring the literature   26

Project: Making a shortlist of possible subjects   34

Project: Selecting your preferred subject   38

Project: Methodology   43

Project: Materials   56

Project and dissertation: Time management and planning   62

Part Three: The 'middle period'
Keeping everything under control   69

Project: Being your own manager   71

Dissertation: Creating your literature review   74

Dissertation: Developing your outline   83

Part Four: The 'end-game'
The challenge to complete   93

Project: Concluding your work   95

Dissertation: Producing your first draft and finalizing your outline   97
Dissertation: Improving your draft   101
Dissertation: Conforming to good academic practice   106
Dissertation: Final editing   118

Notes and references   122

Acknowledgments   123

List of Tables

Table 1: Project and dissertation: Distinctions and parallels   25

Table 2: Details to record about your 'paper' sources   30

Table 3: Types of academic publication   31

Table 4: Project subjects and methodologies   44

Table 5: The 'knowledge content' of materials   58

Table 6: First attempt at dissertation outline   66

Table 7: Using quotations appropriately   78

Table 8: Six general dissertation outlines   84

List of Boxes

Box 1: Choosing your title   33

Box 2: A typical 'to-do' list with time estimates   64

Box 3: Using a word processor   120

Box 4: Queries, feedback, updates, web links   121

Producing a dissertation

READ THIS FIRST!

Are you required, as part of your studies, to submit a dissertation or long essay of 10,000–20,000 words or so? Is it to be created by you alone in your own time and handed in by a specified deadline? Will it be given a mark that counts towards your degree result? If so, this book is for you. But you should also find it helpful if you're working on something longer, like an MPhil or PhD thesis. Much of the advice I offer – e.g. on selecting a subject/topic, creating a literature review, and managing your work – applies whatever the level you're working at.

Many students, faced with the task of producing a dissertation, feel at a loss. They don't know where to start; they feel unprepared for the task. Very largely, I believe, they are in this situation not through any shortcomings of their own but because their experience of education up to that point has indeed not prepared them for the kind of independent work that producing a dissertation calls for. Perhaps this applies to you too. What has been going on?

To answer this question I think we have to look at the 'model' of education to which students are exposed. It seems to me that there are basically two models of education to be found in higher education institutions in the UK, and indeed in UK secondary schools too. In the first model, students are treated as 'receptacles', as containers, to be filled up with knowledge (largely factual knowledge, supplemented with a certain amount of know-how). Courses are 'delivered' to you, and your task is to take in and retain as much of the material in them as you can – and then to reproduce it under examination conditions.

The second model is quite different. In this model, students are treated as 'detectives': you are presented with puzzles and problems to solve, and are expected to acquire not only puzzle-solving and problem-solving techniques but also ways of hunting for and piecing together clues. In other words, you have to acquire not only the necessary techniques but also the initiative, alertness, perceptiveness, intuition and 'sixth sense' that good detectives possess. If you are given coursework assignments to do in your own time, these will test whether you have acquired these 'detective qualities'. However, you will be extremely fortunate if you have teachers who take the trouble to make these explicit and teach them to you. If your teachers don't do this, then your coursework assignments will be testing you on qualities that you haven't actually been taught. If you find yourself getting poor marks for such assignments and don't understand why, that could be the cause.

Here's a thought. Producing a worthwhile dissertation requires you to be a detective. Consequently, if the education you have experienced up to now has given you no training in detective work, it should be no surprise if you feel at a loss when you're required to submit a dissertation. Your experiences as a 'receptacle learner' will be of absolutely no use to you. So do appreciate that you are now in the business of acquiring a new, different method of learning. One of my aims in writing this book is to help you do this.

The book starts from the recognition that producing a dissertation is a twin-track enterprise. It involves both

● undertaking a project: doing the work (including detective work), and

● presenting your findings: writing up your work

and the book is designed to assist you with both these activities. In particular, it is designed to help you *manage* your project work and your writing up.

You may find that you get very little help with the management aspect of producing your dissertation. This may be because the task is regarded as a form of examination, in which you have to work unaided. But even if producing your dissertation is regarded as a learning experience, in which you are entitled to assistance, your supervisor may not be good at giving it.

Academics are not renowned for their management skills, nor for nurturing students who are grappling with tasks that are new to them. You may be fortunate and have a supervisor who is supportive and able to empathize with you when you're struggling. At the other extreme, your supervisor may be completely unable or unwilling to engage with you at an emotional level. If your supervisor is of the latter type, I hope this book may fill the gap to some extent. At the very least, it should provide some reassurance that the problems you face are not unique to you, and some moral support at those inevitable times when your spirits and energy flag.

Every dissertation has to comply with certain requirements. These vary from subject to subject, department to department, and institution to institution. And no dissertation comes into being through exactly the same process. Consequently no worthwhile book of this kind can give 'one size fits all' advice. My approach, therefore, is to highlight the questions that you need to ask to discover for yourself what it is that you have to do, what choices are open to you, and how to choose one course of action rather than another. In a sense, I am offering a compass and other navigational aids to help you find your own way, rather than a map which I am telling you to follow. However, you will find many practical suggestions and recommendations in the following pages.

In the academic world, as in the 'real world' outside, every task is what you make it. You can put a lot of thought and effort into it, or you can put in very little. You could treat 'doing a dissertation' as no more than composing an over-long essay, but something more than that is required for a decent dissertation. Making a précis of six books might just get you a pass mark but it certainly won't win you any prizes. You will need to do something more intellectually demanding: exploring, investigating, testing, analysing, explaining, evaluating, making a critique, and so on. I aim to help you work successfully at this level.

Finally, here are four reasons why it is worth putting some time and effort into creating your dissertation:

- The 'dissertation challenge' offers you an opportunity to get your teeth into a subject that interests you and to pursue it in some depth. It's a chance to step off the week-by-week treadmill that characterizes the majority of academic courses.

- If you feel that conventional examinations are not a good test of your ability, you can take advantage of your dissertation to show what you are capable of.

- A good dissertation will assist your supervisor to write a good reference for you: a sentence or two highlighting the qualities that you've demonstrated will be far more helpful in getting you an interview than some stock phrases about doing well in your studies.

- If you can talk intelligently in an interview about how you tackled your dissertation challenge and what you learned from it, you will be well on the way to being offered the job you're after.

I wish you success!

Peter Levin

Introduction

My overall purpose in writing this book is to help you go about the task of producing a dissertation that will get you an 'excellent' rating in a final-year undergraduate examination or a taught masters examination in the UK. I have been prompted to write this book chiefly by the questions that students working on a dissertation have asked me. For example:

- What are the examiners looking for?
- How should I manage my time?
- My supervisor has told me I have to start by writing a literature review. Is this really the thing I should do first?
- What is my supervisor's responsibility to me?
- How do I structure a dissertation?
- How many chapters should a dissertation have, and how long should they be?
- Which is the best referencing system to use?

The book is divided into four parts, as you can see from the contents pages. Each part is divided into a number of sections. Part One – Preliminaries – deals with things that you need to know before you start. Parts Two, Three and Four deal with the stages you'll be going through: getting started, the 'middle period', and the 'end-game'.

Part One

Preliminaries

Formal requirements and arrangements

Before you start work on producing your dissertation, you *must* do your 'homework' to discover what is officially required of you and what arrangements have been made for supervision, etc. In a sense, this is your first research task, and it needs to be done thoroughly and systematically. Equip yourself with the answers to the questions below.

Documentation and formalities

What documents have been issued to you setting out the requirements to which your dissertation must conform, and what is the status of these documents: are they official university regulations, or guidance notes from your faculty or department? Regulations *must* be complied with – and you are likely to be penalized if you don't comply with them – but guidance notes may merely have the status of advice, with no automatic penalty if you don't follow it.

Purpose

Do the documents you've been given make clear the institution's purpose in requiring you to submit a dissertation? Is it merely a 'take-home' form of examination, one where you pose your own question, set your own time limit, and can write with your books by your side, but get no help from your teachers? Or is the purpose to give you a learning experience, where you have the opportunity to carry out a piece of original research or to delve into a subject more deeply than you have time for on your taught courses, and to get help from your teachers? If the purpose isn't clear, look at the documents you've been given. If they include some kind of statement of 'learning objectives', this suggests the latter purpose, and you should feel entitled to seek the help that is implied.

Marking scheme

In an ideal world, you would be given some guidance as to what the examiners are looking for. This could come in the form of a 'marking scheme', showing what is required for different levels of mark (e.g. pass, merit, distinction at master's level). Or it could be contained in guidance notes that you have received. However, the latter are more likely to specify matters that you should attend to – such as clarity of expression, breadth of literature review, critical appraisal – rather than standards. Where standards *are* implied – e.g. satisfactory abstract, complete and consistent referencing, appropriate research design – you may find them less than helpful in gauging precisely what they mean for you, what actually counts as satisfactory or appropriate. For more on examiners' expectations, see the next section (pages 14–16).

Practicalities

What is the word limit for the dissertation, and does it include or exclude tables, footnotes, appendices and bibliography? Is there any kind of 'format' to which the dissertation is expected to conform? This could cover information to be provided on the title page, page layout (margins, line spacing etc.), and the referencing system to be used.

Handing-in procedure

When and where does the dissertation have to be handed in (submitted): date, time, place? Should you be given a receipt? What are the penalties for handing in late? Examiners are obliged to treat all candidates the same, and this should rule out accepting a late hand-in without penalty unless there are medical or compassionate grounds.

Choice of subject

Are there any limitations as to your subject? Does it have to be one on which there is a substantial body of relevant literature? (And does this literature have to be in English?) Does the subject have to be one which is related to a taught course that you've been following, and/or one which a teacher in your department is willing to supervise? You need to know.

Choice of title

Are you required to submit your dissertation title in advance of the dissertation? If so, what is the procedure to follow? Does your title have to be agreed with your supervisor or anyone else? Does it have to be submitted before you have been assigned to a supervisor, as could be the case if supervisors are appointed on the basis of titles? Will you be able to change it later, or are you stuck with it? You need answers to these questions too.

Supervision

What arrangements are there for supervision? Have you a designated supervisor or tutor, and – if so – what help are you entitled to expect from him or her, and at what stages? If the dissertation is effectively a take-home examination, you may be entitled to expect your supervisor to give assistance in selecting a subject and finding reading matter but not to comment on drafts of your dissertation. If the dissertation is supposed to provide a learning experience, your supervisor may be able to provide guidance with methodology and to comment on early drafts of chapters or sections. Find out if there will be seminars or workshops at which methodology can be discussed and drafts presented.

Assistance

Are you allowed to seek help from other teachers or researchers in your department or elsewhere? This may be a question of what is normal practice in your department or faculty. Or it may be that there are no rules, either formal or informal, in which case ask and see what answer you get.

Access to dissertations written by past students

In some places and some departments you are allowed to see dissertations written by past students; in others you aren't. If you are able to see them, look at several, and make sure you know what grades they have been given: you don't want to take your cue from a poor example. You should treat other people's dissertations as offering you a starting point, no more. Following a past dissertation's treatment slavishly, however good it is, is definitely not a recipe for your success. Every dissertation needs its own, particular, tailor-made treatment.

Consistency

You might like to check that you and your fellow students have all been given the same information and advice. It may be that different supervisors put different interpretations on things, or exercise their discretion differently about how much help to give, or informally give different advice about procedure. There's no harm in satisfying yourself that the playing field is level.

Pleasing the examiners

What examiners like to see

While some examiners do have fixed ideas about how dissertations in their subject should be written, so their standpoint is basically critical, in my experience the majority have an attitude that *appreciates* the qualities to be found in good dissertations. Command of the subject matter is of course essential, but examiners also like to see – and will reward – a dissertation that reveals some or all of the following qualities on the part of the author, the project and/or the dissertation itself:

- The ability to conceive of a purposeful, feasible and manageable project and to frame a concise, meaningful question or questions.

- The ability to choose and apply a clear and appropriate methodology for the project.

- An awareness of the subtleties of the subject, an eye for relevance and significance, and the ability to see connections and to handle a complex subject without oversimplifying it.

- An appreciation of the broad context within which the project is situated: an ability to see both the 'big picture' and significant details.

- Evidence that the relevant literature has been read, digested and appropriately made use of.

- Some evidence of the ability to think independently and critically. 'Originality' may or may not be a requirement for undergraduates and taught postgraduates, although if it is demonstrated it will be appreciated. A dissertation containing original work will usually be awarded a merit or distinction.

- Thoroughness: evidence that work has been done carefully; that proper attention has been given to detail; that the subject has been treated comprehensively (e.g. no omissions in its coverage, no significant aspects left unexplored); and that the study has been properly completed (no loose ends remaining).

- A systematic, logical and appropriate structure for the dissertation.

- Persuasive advocacy in subjects where you are expected to put forward a point of view and argue for it.

- Evidence that the dissertation is indeed the work of the person submitting it.

- Compliance with the formal requirements. Failure to comply with the word limit or hand in by the deadline will usually result in a penalty: loss of marks, or worse.

What examiners don't like to see

You should also be aware of what, in general, examiners *don't* like to see:

- Use of your own personal experience ('anecdotal evidence') unless you treat it in a rigorous manner.

- Use of the words 'I think' or 'I believe'. Statements of your thoughts and beliefs do not constitute valid elements of reasoning in an academic dissertation. If your thoughts are based on evidence, as they should be, offer this evidence and demonstrate what follows from it. Likewise, if your beliefs are based on certain values, make these explicit.

- Straying outside your discipline. While taking a technique that has been developed in one academic field and applying it in another may demonstrate that you are a gifted lateral thinker, this may not be appreciated by the examiners. If you are an economist, you will almost certainly be expected to deploy the techniques and reasoning of an economist, not those of a sociologist or psychologist, for example. Likewise, if you are an archaeology graduate who is doing a masters in anthropology, it may well be prudent to keep your archaeological knowledge and training well in the background. But do check with your supervisor whether this is the case. There are a few enlightened academics who recognize the benefits of taking of a cross-disciplinary approach to a subject, but unfortunately many do not.

- Poor use of English, especially if the result is that the meaning of what you write is not clear. Your writing in English does not have to be sophisticated or elegant, but you must use words accurately – i.e. you must use the correct word for the meaning you want to convey – and your grammar, punctuation and spelling must be acceptable to the examiners. 'Chatty' language and slang will not be appreciated.

You and your supervisor

Rights and expectations

There should be a code of practice in your institution that sets out your rights with regard to supervision. Usually such a code will cover your progress and performance in the whole range of your academic studies, including your dissertation work. Your rights may be expressed in the form of a statement of your supervisor's duties towards you, the word 'rights' not being mentioned. Such a code may also imply expectations without expressing them as rights: look out for statements like 'Supervisors also undertake a pastoral role ...' which do this.

But you and your supervisor are both human beings, and there are limits as to how far 'one-to-one' human interactions can be 'legislated for'. It follows that if there is to be a relationship between you that is helpful to you, even if your supervisor is available to you only while you're choosing your subject, you may have to take an active part in creating it.

Observe your supervisor

A good rule is to observe your supervisor carefully, from the moment you first meet him or her. Is this someone who sees their role as that of 'guide, philosopher and friend'? Someone who takes the trouble to put you at your ease, who listens attentively to your concerns, and doesn't end a meeting before you have agreed when you will next meet and what work you will do before your next meeting? Such people do exist, and they can make being supervised a very rewarding experience.

But keep asking questions. Is this someone who has their own agenda with regard to choosing a subject? Someone who is clearly anxious to get meetings over quickly? Someone who doesn't probe areas where you express uncertainty? Who gets embarrassed if you talk about personal matters? Or who behaves in a warmer and friendlier manner than you feel is appropriate?

Formulate your tactics

If your experiences with your supervisor are consistently negative, to the extent where you feel you have no confidence in him or her, you may be able to request a transfer: your institution should have a formal procedure for this. But you should do what you can to avoid matters getting to such a point. Here are a few suggestions:

- Don't take things personally. If your supervisor is a self-centred obsessive, preoccupied with his or her own research as many academics are (indeed, as they have to be if they are to fulfil the targets set for them in today's academic world), their behaviour won't be the result of any antagonism towards you specially.

- Identify your supervisor's strengths and take advantage of them. If he or she isn't much good at providing encouragement and sympathy but is an expert in their field, use them as a consultant. See if you can find someone else – a friendly academic, a fellow student or a group of fellow students – who can provide you with the emotional support that everyone who's working on a project and dissertation needs at some point.

● If your supervisor does have 'consultant qualities', the way to get his or her attention is to intrigue them. So before a meeting do as much preparatory work – reading, investigating, thinking – as you can, and try to come up with a dilemma or puzzle that will challenge them. Seek their advice on it. Whatever you do, don't act helpless. Don't ask to be told what to do. Your supervisor isn't your parent or even your instructor.

● It may be that the person appointed as your supervisor is not a specialist in your chosen subject. Perhaps you have chosen a subject in which there are no specialists in your department, or there is a specialist but he or she is unavailable. Don't kick yourself for not having chosen a different subject. While non-specialists won't be acquainted with all the relevant literature, they will often be able to help with methodology and planning, and their experience in the wider field may make them good people to try your ideas out on. They're also less likely to be offended if you go and pick the brains of experts elsewhere.

● During meetings with your supervisor, take notes. As soon as possible after each meeting, write them up, so you have a record of the advice given and any agreements reached and decisions taken. It does sometimes happen that supervisors forget what they told you at a previous meeting and give advice that contradicts advice they gave earlier. Having a record will help you to resolve such contradictions. And if, unhappily, your relationship with your supervisor does break down, your records will strengthen your hand and your case when you seek to remedy the situation.

Part Two

Getting started

The 'twin-track': Your project and your dissertation

The distinction between project and dissertation

In creating a dissertation, you have two things to do. You must:

- Undertake a project: for example, a project to find the answer to a research question, to test a theory or hypothesis, to evaluate an action or proposal, to formulate a critique.

- Write up your project in the form of a dissertation, in which you present your findings, discuss their significance and offer your conclusions.

It is easy to lose sight of the distinction between project and dissertation, between undertaking your project and writing it up. If you think of your task as being to *write* a dissertation, or to *author* a thesis, you are already blurring that distinction: you're losing sight of the fact that you have a project to do. Likewise, if your project is one of reading and thinking (as in history, law or philosophy) rather than fieldwork or laboratory work, you could easily lose sight of the distinction, because writing will be part of your project work as well as your writing up.

It may help to distinguish between 'writing as thinking' (part of your project work) and 'writing as assembly job' (putting your presentation together), and in this book I'll be reminding you here and there to do this. I'll also be suggesting that you make it easier for yourself to move from project to dissertation by writing notes to yourself during your project work. These notes will give you a flying start when you get to the writing-up stage: you will be able to assemble much of your first draft out of them.

Oddly, the distinction between project and dissertation seems to be lost on some academics and institutions. You can see this from the emphasis that they put on dissertation titles. You may be told to suggest a title to your supervisor and to discuss it with him or her, and formally to submit your proposed title to your institution, but may not be invited to discuss the subject and methodology of your project in any detail. This despite the fact that you can't possibly be clear about the suitability of a title unless you have first clarified your thoughts about the project you intend to undertake and checked out its feasibility.

Project and dissertation usually develop together. Most students find not only that their project work feeds into their dissertation, as you would expect, but also that the process of writing up generates thoughts and ideas which feed into their project. So don't feel that you have to complete your project before you do any writing. It will pay you to keep asking yourself, while you are doing your project: 'What shall I be able to write about this? What will it contribute to my dissertation?'

There are some important distinctions and parallels between project and dissertation: these are shown in Table 1.

While your project and dissertation will 'grow up' together, in some respects the project must come first, of course. You have to do some work before you have anything to write up. You have to be clear what your subject and methodology are before you can arrive at your title. And you must be reasonably clear about your plan of work before you can rough out a plan for your dissertation.

At the same time, though, you must bear in mind the dissertation requirements while planning your project. The deadline and the word limit for the dissertation will limit the scope of your project. And your dissertation

Table 1: Project and dissertation: distinctions and parallels

	Project	Dissertation
Activity	Doing the work (including reading, thinking and formulating thoughts on paper)	Writing up your work and presenting your writing in a logical and readable format
Focus/keynote	Subject (the situation, event, phenomenon, theory, theme or whatever that you are studying) and approach	Title. You may also find the word 'topic' used in connection with your dissertation as a synonym for 'subject'
Structure	Your plan of work	The outline (plan) of your dissertation: chapter and section headings

will need to incorporate a discussion and conclusions, so it is important to design your project to maximize the likelihood that you will come up with results that you can report and interpret in your discussion and conclusions.

First steps

The first steps towards producing your dissertation require you to do a number of things. You have to explore the literature, make a shortlist of possible subjects for your project, select your preferred subject, think about the methodology you will use and the materials that you will apply your methodology to, and devote some thought to time management and planning. The following sections of this part of the book deal with these in turn.

Project and dissertation: Exploring the literature

By 'the literature' I mean academic publications: books, articles and theses or dissertations by academics or other scholars. I'm not including in this category official and other formal publications, or data sources and reference handbooks, or writings that constitute the subject matter of your project: these all come under the heading of 'materials', and I deal with them later on (pages 56–61).

How to read

Reading causes huge problems to many students. Several factors contribute to this. One is that when they come to university they take it for granted that they already know what 'reading' is and how to do it: you open a book at page 1, start reading, and keep going –

word by word, sentence by sentence, paragraph by paragraph and chapter by chapter – until you've reached the end, when you can stop. A second factor that makes reading problematic is the sheer quantity of literature that exists today on most subjects; and a third factor is that much of this literature is written in 'academic-speak', the specialist language used by academics in that field.

Given that academic learning is largely 'driven' by the written word, when you're faced with this mass of literature, what can you do? As I've suggested in *Write great essays!*, the first thing you must do is to 'reframe' your notion of what 'reading' is. Think of it not as soaking up great masses of stuff, but as conducting a kind of treasure hunt to find the specific points that you need. And the second thing you must do is to explore the literature, systematically.

Exploring the literature is different from writing a literature review. Don't confuse the two. Writing a literature review involves writing an essay that presents an overview of the relevant literature and brings out points that are important for your project. (For more on writing a literature review, see pages 74–82.) But exploring the literature is a matter of discovering what there is and what you might use. So you're searching for sources, acquainting yourself with what is in them, looking out for potentially useful information, concepts, theories and background material. Don't try to master the literature until you're clearer what you want each publication *for*.

Track down potentially useful academic publications

Here are some ideas to help you track down potentially useful academic publications:

- Make the most of any relevant reading lists that you have been given for your taught courses. Starting with the most recent publications listed, check out their references and bibliographies for leads to other books and articles.

- Make full use of your institution's library. Take advantage of any courses it runs in how to find useful publications, and consult the enquiry or help desk when you need assistance in finding your way around. If you haven't already done so, learn to use its computerized catalogue, and find out whether its computer system allows you to search for publications on your particular subject.

● Find out what specialist libraries there are in your field – many professional institutes and institutions maintain libraries at their headquarters – and investigate the possibility of gaining access to them. A student card and/or a letter from your head of department or supervisor may be needed for them to let you in. They may well have journals that your institution's library doesn't.

● Identify the most relevant journals in your field and browse through recent numbers, checking out not only articles but also book reviews and letters to the editor for mentions of your subject.

● If there are prominent writers on your subject, look them up on a search engine, such as Google or Google Scholar. You might find a reference to a recent paper, or a recent or forthcoming lecture or conference appearance, that's worth following up.

There are no short cuts. Don't expect anyone else to do this work for you. Once you've done some scouting around – but not before – consult your supervisor to see if there's anything you've missed. You are much more likely to get useful help if you have already shown some initiative. The same applies if you want to consult experts elsewhere. A letter or email along the lines 'I am making a study of ... What should I read?' is likely to go straight into the waste paper basket (trash).

Start compiling a bibliography and collecting publications

A dissertation's bibliography is a list of the publications consulted by the writer. Every dissertation must have one. Start compiling yours straight away. Every time you come across a potentially useful publication, add it to your list. (See Table 2 on page 30 for the details of each publication that you need to make a note of. Do be sure to write down full details of each one: it can be a frustrating business trying to recapture these details later.) You can always delete items from your list in the writing-up stage if you end up not having used them.

Students tackling a dissertation project invariably find themselves building up and using a collection of publications on their subject. Understandably so: it is a common experience that as you learn more and think more about your subject, you keep returning to your collection of publications, and each time you do so you see things that didn't register with you when you read them before.

So don't rely on being able to find publications in the library when you want them, or on web pages always being available (and available in the form they had when you first found them), and don't try to skimp on publications: it will almost certainly turn out to be a false economy. Set aside some funds for buying books, photocopying chapters and articles, and printing out material you've downloaded from the web. Once you've chosen your subject, start collecting. Incidentally, if you're photocopying a chapter from a book, check whether there is anything potentially useful in other chapters, such as the introduction and conclusions: you may want to photocopy those too.

You are of course free to highlight, underline, sideline and make marginal comments on any books or papers that are your own personal property, and I do encourage you to do that. (If you've been well brought up and it goes against the grain to mark a book, use pencil – so you can erase it later – and semi-sticky labels: Post-its make excellent bookmarks.) You'll find it's a great help in digesting the material and ultimately making the subject 'yours'.

Record details of publications

Citing sources will be easier to do if you make a habit of recording their details at the time when you take notes from them. When you're photocopying pages from a book save yourself some work by photocopying the title page too, because it will have some of the details you need (don't forget to add the year of publication and number of edition to your photocopied title page). In Table 2 I list the details you'll need to record about 'paper' sources, i.e. books and articles.

Table 2: Details to record about your 'paper' sources

For a 'unitary' book (i.e. written as a whole, not an edited compilation)	For a chapter in an edited compilation book	For an article in a journal
The name(s) of the author(s)	The name(s) of the author(s) of the chapter	The name(s) of the author(s)
The title and subtitle	The title of the chapter	The title of the article
The year of publication	The title and subtitle of the book	The title of the journal and any standard abbreviation of the title
The edition, if not the first	The name(s) of the editor(s) of the book	The year of publication
The publisher	The year of publication	The number of the volume of the journal
The city or town and state (in USA) where the publisher's main office is situated	The publisher	The part number of the journal and the month (or season) of publication
The number(s) of the relevant pages	The city or town and state (in USA) where the publisher's main office is situated	The number(s) of the relevant pages
	The number(s) of the relevant pages	

For an item on a web page you will need to record

● The URL (uniform resource locator) of the page, otherwise known as its web address.

● The date on which you accessed the page.

It is sensible to copy and paste the URL into a document to guard against errors in copying by hand, especially if the URL is one of those monster database-generated ones whose rhyme and reason are known only to the webmaster.

And be sure to store the web page electronically, and also to print it out, so you have it to refer to if the page is subsequently altered or becomes unavailable. And watch out for line breaks (*never* insert a hyphen, as this will change the URL) and for underscores concealed by an underline.

Make a list of sources and annotate it

When you come across a publication that's new to you, it's very easy to be intimidated by it, to see no way of taking a critical approach to it. One thing you can do to help yourself 'get a handle on it' is to ask what 'type' of publication it is. Use the list of types of academic publication in Table 3 to do this.

Table 3: Types of academic publication

Publication type	Description
Question-to-Answer	Starts with a question and concludes with the answer to it. Answers range from plausible speculation to rigorous explanation in terms of theories and mechanisms
Research report	The story of what the author did and found
Review	Reviews research findings, literature, 'state of the art', current debate, etc., in a field
Theory	Presents a conceptual framework of some kind and its implications
Argument	Argues/puts the case for a particular opinion
Issue-centred	Starts with an issue (a 'What should be done?' question) and usually concludes by advocating a particular course of action
Thematic	Is constructed around a 'theme', and incorporates elements of some or all of the above
Compilation	Contains elements of some or all of the above
Textbook	Contains elements of some or all of the above, especially survey and theory, tailored to a student readership
Methodology texts	Books on how to do research, statistical methods, etc. Almost all research reports also contain descriptions of the methodology employed

When exploring the literature, all you want to know is whether a publication that you come across might be useful to you. When you find something that you think is potentially useful, write a little note to yourself, giving the details of the publication (as in Table 2); the type of publication (as in Table 3), if it's an academic one; any comments on it that come to mind; and your thoughts on how you might make use of it. File your note in a folder or ring-binder labelled 'literature'.

Don't start writing your literature review yet

At this early stage, do not spend valuable time starting to write your literature review. It's possible that your supervisor will ask you to show him or her a literature review early on, but try to get out of this. There are three reasons for avoiding this task. First, you don't know, when you're starting work, which pieces of literature will be relevant to your future work and which ones will not. Second, you are quite likely to uncover fresh sources as your work proceeds: it is not a good use of your time to redo work each time you find a new source. Third, it is only when you are well advanced that you will be able to be properly critical of the books and articles that you are using. Writing a literature review when you aren't yet on top of your material is one of the most mind-numbing, brain-deadening, sleep-inducing activities known to students. If your supervisor is insistent, try to get away with producing just a list of sources and a brief note on the content and possible value of each.

Box 1

Choosing your title

Once you've begun thinking about your subject start to draw up a shortlist of alternative titles, especially if you are able or required to discuss your title with your supervisor. You will get a more useful reaction if you offer a selection than if you offer only one.

If you like the idea of a snazzy, eye-catching title, take advantage of the 'colon convention' that allows you to have a double title, with the two parts separated by a colon, e.g. 'Manners makyth man: a cross-cultural study of social etiquette at ballroom dances'.

If you have to submit your title at an early stage and won't have the opportunity later to change it, make sure you choose one that is not too restrictive, so it can accommodate changes in direction or emphasis that you may later find necessary. For example, 'Local democracy in the United Kingdom: a case study' offers more room for manoeuvre than 'Local by-elections in the London Borough of Newham 1998–2002'.

Project: Making a shortlist of possible subjects

What grabs you?

What do you actually want to do for your dissertation project? Most people start from a general idea about the subject they want to tackle. They say things like 'It would be interesting to look at the Human Rights Act 1998' or 'I'd like to write about the Crimean war'. Statements like these are not specific enough to get you going – they say nothing about the approach you're going to adopt – but they do give you a starting point. What will *your* starting point be?

The formal requirements for your dissertation will impose some limitations on your choice of subject. You will certainly be required to produce a dissertation that is your own work, and it would be sensible not to take a subject that you know someone else has taken unless your approach would be different and/or you have good grounds for thinking that you would come up with different results and conclusions. Your subject does not need to be one that no one anywhere has ever tackled before, and your dissertation ought not be judged on whether it makes an original contribution to knowledge (that's for a PhD), but in practice it is almost certainly worth trying to find a combination of subject and approach that breaks some new ground. Below are some questions to get you thinking along those lines. At this stage, don't worry about how to choose a single subject: concentrate for now on drawing up a shortlist of possibles. Anything from two to five will be a good number.

- Is there something that you've come across in one of your taught courses that you didn't have time to explore properly but would like to know more about? Have you ever asked a teacher a question and not been satisfied with the answer? Now's your chance to see if you can put together a better one. Checking out past exam papers might give you an idea or two.

- What's currently happening in your field of study? In most fields there's usually something new or recent to be investigated. Is there a new book or article with new ideas, the implications of which you would like to explore? Is there a disagreement, with protagonists expressing different points of view? This offers scope for exploring how it is possible for different views to be held and the possibility of reconciling them. Has a new theory been published, one that you could test? Has a new technique become available, one that you could compare with or apply alongside existing techniques? If a new product has become available, could you explore its properties and evaluate its usefulness?

- Has a new source of data become available, offering a rich vein of material for analysis? Do you have contacts outside university giving you access to materials to which you could apply methodologies that you have learned?

- Has someone published a case study which it would be interesting to replicate in a different context, allowing you to compare its findings with your own and to test – and possibly refine – their methodology?

- Is there some literature in your field that you are critical of, or a train of thought you would like to pursue? Do you feel you have something to contribute to a current debate? Or is there a gap of some kind that you think you could fill? (A gap by itself may not be very inspiring, however: see if you can formulate a question or puzzle that would help you to fill it.)

- Do you have some personal experience that you would like to draw on? This is legitimate, and will certainly help you to meet any requirement to do with originality, but there are traps that you must avoid. You must not merely give an account of your experience but place it in the context of other studies and/or theories. And you must avoid being judgmental: confine your judgments to your discussion and conclusions, and make clear if you can the values on which they are based. It's a good idea to take other people's experiences as your subject, and draw on your own to give you insights into their experiences.

- If you're an international student in a social science field, would it be interesting – and feasible – to make a comparative study between your home country and the UK, or to investigate a UK-centred subject which would generate useful lessons that you could take home with you?

Two warnings

A word of warning. Avoid subjects set in the future, like 'What will happen if/when …?' The future is not susceptible of investigation, and although you may be able to get somewhere by extrapolating into the future you'll get very few if any marks for speculating about it.

Another word of warning: do not let your supervisor talk you into taking on a subject that you are not comfortable with. (Unless, of course, you want to find out at first hand what it's like to have a nervous breakdown.) Students do sometimes think that their supervisor knows best, and take his or her advice despite their own misgivings, especially if they are taking a Master's in a field different from that of their Bachelor's degree. But supervisors often have their own agendas and some are not at all good at putting themselves in a student's shoes. Get as much informed advice as you can (or can accommodate: too much advice can be very inhibiting) but at the end of the day trust your own instincts and make your own decision.

▼ ▼ ▼

At the end of this exercise you should have a shortlist of two to five possible subjects. They can be quite general at this stage. Once you have your shortlist, you can start thinking about which to choose. That's the subject of the next section.

Project: Selecting your preferred subject

Checklist for selecting

Given your shortlist of possible subjects, you have to make a choice between them. Before you can do this, though, you must do some work on each of them. Here is a checklist of six questions to ask about each possible subject: for the one you end up choosing, you need to be able to answer 'yes' to all six of them:

- Is this subject specific enough?
- Is this subject narrow enough?
- Do I have a clear aim?
- Do I have a feasible approach to this subject?
- Is there a good chance that I'll come up with an interesting conclusion?
- Am I enthusiastic about this subject?

Make your subject specific

It's very likely that if you have identified a possible subject in general terms, you are thinking of it in quite 'woolly' language, in academic-speak. You need to express it in specific, 'concrete' terms. So translate all academic-speak words into down-to-earth language: describe your subject in terms that will enable anyone to recognize it when they see it.

Narrow your subject down

Narrowing a subject down involves setting boundaries to it. This might involve limiting it to one or two particular case studies, geographical areas, historical periods, organizations, physical phenomena, writers, or socio-economic groups, for example. Bear in mind the unavoidable trade-off between breadth and depth: the broader your subject, the shallower your project will inevitably be.

For example, take the question that students often ask: How many case studies should I make? Consider the options: one, two or three. Tackling just one case study will allow you to go into greatest depth. This might be particularly good for testing a theory: it takes only one demonstration that the theory does not hold to invalidate it. It might also be particularly good for generating insights into the mechanisms, say, that the proponents of this theory seek to explain. Tackling two case studies must have the effect of reducing the depth that you can go into, because your time and the number of words permitted are limited. On the other hand, it will allow you to make comparisons between the two, if they have some features in common, and you can explore the use of the theory in explaining the differences that you discover. Tackling three case studies will reduce your depth even more, although it could yield some more interesting comparisons: you will have to make your own judgment as to whether the loss of depth is outweighed by the gain in breadth.

Identify a clear aim

Identifying a clear aim involves getting it clear in your mind what it is that you want to learn about your subject.

Identify a feasible approach

Identifying a feasible approach to your subject requires you to ensure that you have a methodology (see pages 43–55) that will enable you to achieve your aim, the materials to which you can apply your methodology (see pages 56–61), and the personal resources (such as time and ability) that you will need.

Envisage arriving at an interesting conclusion

It will be very helpful if you can visualize, in at least a broad outline, an interesting conclusion that you might come to, and get some indication from your supervisor that that conclusion is likely to arouse the examiners' interest.

Be enthused by your subject

Whatever the subject you choose, it's really important that you have some enthusiasm for it. Producing a dissertation is hard work, and you'll need some enthusiasm to sustain you when the going gets tough.

An example

For example, you might be saying to yourself 'I want to consider the issues that professionalization in social work addresses'. Now apply the six questions in the above checklist.

Is this subject specific enough? No. The words 'issues', 'professionalization' and 'addresses' are abstract academic-speak: before you can work out how you are going to undertake your project they have to be translated into specific, 'concrete' terms. That is to say, you have to be able to say how you distinguish 'issues' when you see them, or at least to give some concrete examples of issues. Similarly with 'professionalization' (which could mean either the state of 'being professional' or the process of 'becoming professional') and 'addresses'.

Is this subject narrow enough? No. As it stands it is far too broad, because it is so unspecific.

Do I have a clear aim? No. All you've said is that you're going to 'consider' issues: this could amount to nothing more than producing a stream of commentary – possibly mere 'waffle' – on the subject. It conveys nothing at all about what you want to learn.

Do I have a feasible approach to this subject? Without a specific subject and a clear aim, it's not possible to draw up a feasible approach.

Is there a good chance that I'll come up with an interesting conclusion? It's impossible to say.

Am I enthusiastic about this subject? In my experience, people who cannot give clear and positive answers to the first five questions tend to be depressed rather than enthusiastic about their project.

Let's try again.

A more specific subject. A more specific formulation of your subject could be: (a) actions taken at national and local level in the past ten years directed towards raising the professional standards of members of the social work profession; and (b) the number of cases of children placed on at-risk registers in the past ten years who have subsequently suffered a non-accidental injury.

A narrow enough subject. Being more specific, your subject is already narrower, but you will probably need to narrow it down further by confining yourself to one or two regions or localities.

A clear aim. You're asking a clear question: Is there a correlation between the actions taken to raise the professional standards of members of the social work profession and the number of children placed on at-risk registers who subsequently suffered a non-accidental injury. And you would be asking a clear subsequent question: What has brought about the correlation or lack of it that you find?

A feasible approach. To judge whether your approach is feasible you will need to know at the very least whether (a) you can identify actions that have actually been taken to raise professional standards: this may depend on whether these have been documented and, if so, on whether you can gain access to the relevant documentation; and (b) you can gain access to the data you need on the children with whom you are concerned. Your search for an explanation of your findings would probably involve interviewing people: you would need to be sure you have the time and skills needed to arrange and carry out interviews, transcribe your notes and compile a report on them.

The chance that you will come up with an interesting conclusion. Whether you find a correlation or not, I think you could well have something interesting to report and something worth trying to explain.

Am I enthusiastic about this subject? Certainly you now have more grounds for enthusiasm.

Make your choice

If you have started off with a shortlist of possible subjects, my suggestion is that you ask the six questions in the checklist about each of them. Then compare your lists and make a choice. If this is difficult, ask your supervisor for help. Even if it seems straightforward, it will be worthwhile asking for comments. Your supervisor may well be able to point out aspects that haven't occurred to you. The fact that you have done your homework first will help to get you a sympathetic hearing.

When you have chosen your subject, write yourself a note with your answers to the checklist questions above. So it should cover: description of subject (must be specific enough); boundaries of subject (must be narrow enough); aims (must be clear enough); feasibility (must be doable); reasons for thinking there's a good chance of an interesting conclusion; and why you feel enthusiastic about this project. Pin this note up somewhere where you'll see it every time you sit down to work. Update it whenever you change something. You'll find it useful in keeping yourself on track, and particularly valuable when you come to write the Introduction to your dissertation.

Project: Methodology

To carry out a project successfully, you must be absolutely clear what methodology you are using, and how you are using it. (I use the word 'methodology' to denote principles and ways of working as well as specific methods and techniques.) It is beyond the scope of this book to go in any detail into the methodologies employed by the whole range of academic disciplines. However, if you are to make a success of managing your project there are certain general questions about methodology to which you must have satisfactory answers. In this section I distinguish different kinds of subject and the methodologies that go with them, and set out a checklist of questions to ask about each of them.

Kinds of subject and the methodologies that go with them

There are several kinds of subject. Each calls for its own particular methodology. I have listed these in Table 4.

Table 4: Project subjects and methodologies

Subject	Methodology (what you do)
A phenomenon, natural or man-made, such as an event, a situation, a process, or the behaviour of an individual or group	Investigate it, describe it, and seek to explain it
A theory, theoretical model, 'law' or hypothesis	Test it
A proposition or philosophical argument	Test it
A design, proposal, action or technique	Evaluate it
An issue or problem	Explore it and, if possible, (re)solve it
A creative work	Analyse it and make a critique of it
A theme	Discuss it
A thesis	Argue in support of it

Investigating, describing and explaining a phenomenon

The phenomenon that you wish to investigate may already be – or have been – in existence, or it may be one that you yourself manufacture, as when you carry out an experiment. For example, you can carry out an experiment to find out what happens if you heat a substance up to a high temperature, or cool it down to a low temperature, or pass an electric current through it. And you can create a particular physical environment and see how different people respond when placed in it.

Before you can investigate a phenomenon you must have at least some description of it. There must be features of it that have registered with you.

And your description must be concrete enough to enable you to recognize it when you see it. An academic-speak description won't do. If you describe your phenomenon as 'international trade in goods and commodities', or 'the effect on one financial market of events in another', you have something that you can recognize. If you describe it as 'globalization', you don't.

When we describe a phenomenon, we do so by picking out those features which strike us as 'salient', as having significance. Ask two people to go into a room, one after the other, and then to come out and describe the room, and they will give different descriptions. To one, the large number of books and office equipment will be the salient features. To another, the salient features will be the low ceiling and smoky atmosphere. If you wish to embark on explaining a phenomenon, it is likely that the features of it which are salient for you are ones which pose a puzzle of some kind.

Puzzles mostly come into our minds in the form of questions. For example: 'Why did X happen?' 'Why did it take the form that it did?' 'Why did it happen when it did?' There are three things to note about such questions. First, there is a presumption of causation, that something *caused* X to happen, and to happen in the form that it did and when it did. Second, such questions come into our minds against the background of other knowledge that we already have. These three questions all incorporate pre-suppositions, drawn from this other knowledge: that X might not have happened, that it might have taken a different form, that it might have happened at a different time. And third, these presuppositions draw us into the realm of 'counterfactuals': *we are working with the infinity of events and combinations of events that did not happen.*

Faced with such puzzles, physical and natural scientists behave differently from social scientists. The former do operate on the presumption of causation, in a 'tight' form – they presume that something *determined* that X would happen – but they minimize the part that presuppositions and counterfactuals can play in their thinking. They do this (a) by isolating the phenomenon, as far as possible; (b) by ensuring where possible that they can reproduce it, so they know their initial observations were not the result of an accident; (c) by controlling the conditions and changing only one independent variable at a time while keeping all the others constant; and (d) by focusing on relating their observations to established theories about the mechanisms to be found in their subject of study. When they ask questions of the form 'Why did X happen?', they seek for *consistency* between their observations and established facts and theories. If they find the consistency they're looking for, they consider that they have explained why X happened.

The procedure is very similar if they start by asking open-ended questions of the form 'What will happen if ...?': they conduct an experiment to see what X results, and then seek to explain it in the same way. Or, using theory, they consciously make predictions – 'If we do V, X should happen' – and then see whether their predictions are fulfilled: if so, they have attained the consistency and thus the explanation they seek.

In short, by taking consistency between observations and established facts and theories as the acid test of 'explanation', and by adopting a methodology in which counterfactuals play little or no part, physical and natural scientists make their task a manageable one.

In the humanities and social sciences, explanation is much more difficult. Mostly, phenomena cannot be isolated; exact reproducibility is very difficult or impossible to attain; it is difficult or impossible to control conditions; and theories as to the mechanisms at work are, in many fields, primitive. This last point is crucial. As a student, you will find that you are asked 'Why?' questions, which implicitly call for an explanation, but you are not offered any concept of 'explanation' or given any criterion for judging whether an 'explanation' offered to you is a good one or not. (If any criterion at all is made explicit, it is likely to be 'plausibility' rather than consistency.)[1] Your teachers draw your attention to 'factors' that may have had a causal effect, but not to the mechanisms by which these factors operate. You are likely to be asked counterfactual questions – for example: 'Why did China not industrialize earlier than it did?' – but not taught how to deal with such questions. In attempting to answer them you find yourself speculating about might-have-beens, and it is very easy for experienced academics to pick holes in your work. Moreover, you are liable to be asked a question and at the same time told you have to produce an 'argument': a sure-fire recipe for writer's block because an argument is not an answer to a question. In your project you may well have reasoned your way step by step from question to answer, from starting point to conclusion, but in your dissertation you are expected to start from your conclusion and then present evidence, opinions etc. that back it up. So the structure of your dissertation is diametrically at odds with the structure of your reasoning process.

While it cannot be disputed that social, political, economic and cultural phenomena are almost always the outcome of a complicated set of situational factors and mechanisms, and that it is much more difficult to conduct controlled experiments, the physical sciences do offer some lessons to any humanities or social science student who wants to investigate, describe and explain a phenomenon. Here are some suggestions:

- Try as far as possible to avoid counterfactuals in any form. Try not to make conjectures about 'might-have-beens'. Aim to make comparative studies of phenomena, so you are dealing with sets of concrete observations. Two case studies will generally be superior to one for that reason, but – as we saw on page 39 – because of time constraints and the word limit on your dissertation you may not be able to go into as much depth with two as you can with one. And if you are thinking about undertaking three case studies, take into account the further reduction in depth you will have to accept.

- Keep your study as simple as possible. Resist the temptation, to which many students succumb, to enquire into 'causes and consequences'. Causes usually will give you quite enough to keep you occupied. Consequences take you into the realm of counterfactuals, because you are comparing what did happen after the event (say) with what might have occurred if the event had not happened.

- Aim to use several investigative methods in conjunction with one another. It can be very rewarding to use in conjunction the tools of economics, sociology, psychology, geography and political science to investigate a behavioural phenomenon (your supervisor permitting). And if you are carrying out a large-scale data-collection survey, complement it with a smaller, focused interview survey to give yourself deeper insights into the phenomenon you are investigating. If you are using one technique that reveals a correlation between two variables, use another to investigate possible cause-and-effect connections.

- If you are aiming to explain a phenomenon, it is bad practice to ignore any potentially relevant theory or facts. Don't impose any arbitrary exclusions or limits.

- If you are thinking about cause-and-effect relationships in terms of causal factors, try to distinguish between factors of different kinds. For example, you may be able to identify (a) 'triggering' factors which precipitated a sequence of events; (b) factors that promoted an event and factors that enabled it; (c) 'necessary' and/or 'sufficient' conditions for an event to have occurred ('necessary' implies that in the absence of the condition the event could not have occurred; 'sufficient' implies that if the condition had been present no other conditions needed to be present for the event to occur); and/or (d) considerations of motivation, opportunity and resources that entered into the rationale behind certain decisions.

- Whatever the phenomenon that you are working on, think about mechanisms. Ask yourself what mechanisms are at work and do your best to uncover them.

- While you should do what you can to be objective – don't ask leading questions when you're interviewing people, don't make your mind up about anything before you've considered all the evidence – you should feel encouraged to question received wisdom. Arguably, objectivity is nothing more than the sum total of subjectivities that all agree with one another.

Testing a theory, theoretical model, 'law' or hypothesis

Before you can test a theory (say), you must be clear what it is claimed that the theory does. Most theories, theoretical models, 'laws' and hypotheses are about relationships between variables. There are others – for example, hypotheses that amount to nothing more than conjectures, such as the conjecture that it will rain tomorrow – but these are not suitable subjects for an academic dissertation. So confine your attention to a theory that can be expressed *either*

- in the form of a relationship that links dependent and independent variables: if the values of the independent ones are changed, the values of the dependent ones will necessarily change too, to new ones that are determined by the new values of the independent variables, *or*

- in the form of an assertion that if certain conditions are (or were) present, the introduction of a disturbance – e.g. a force of some kind, a stimulus, an alien body or an innovation – will (or did) inevitably have a certain outcome: here the precise connection between conditions, disturbance and outcome is left unstated. Such assertions are sometimes expressed in a weaker form, with 'will tend to have' taking the place of 'will inevitably have'.

A theory makes a suitable subject for a project if you are able to test it (your supervisor may say 'evaluate it') in some way. Before testing it, you must have a clear and precise statement of it. Once you have that, there are two main possibilities for testing: empirical testing and inspection.

Empirical testing is carried out by making observations in the 'real world'. You should aim to make observations that would help you to answer the following questions:

- Is this theory consistent with other observations that I have already made or facts that I am aware of? If not, either the theory fails the test or the observations/'facts' are not to be relied on.

- Does this theoretical model or 'law', which was originally formulated and found to hold in a particular set of real-world circumstances (conditions), hold in others? If not, the model will need to be elaborated or qualified.

- If this hypothesis holds, what can I predict, and how will I know whether the prediction is accurate? The acid test of a hypothesis is whether it enables predictions to be made and checked against reality. If the prediction is not fulfilled, the hypothesis fails: it is not valid (tenable).

Inspection can be carried out without leaving your desk. For example, you can ask:

- Is this theory internally consistent, i.e. free from internal contradictions? If not, the theory is unsound.

- Is this theory consistent with other theories? If not, either the theory or one or more of the other theories is unsound.

- Are the assumptions on which this theory is said to be based valid ones? If not, either the theory is unsound or its soundness does not actually depend on those assumptions being valid.

Testing a proposition or philosophical argument

To test a proposition, P, or a philosophical argument, you must first of all have a clear statement of the proposition or argument. Once you have this, and before you do anything else, unpick it: break it down into its component parts. If you are dealing with an argument, make a list of the steps in the chain of reasoning.

As in the case of testing a theory, there are a number of questions that you can use as starting points. For example:

● On what axioms, postulates or suppositions does P rest? Can these be regarded as valid? If not, P is not valid.

● Is each step in the chain of reasoning logically sound? If not, the argument is faulty.

● If P is accepted as valid ('true'), what consequences follow logically from that? Investigating these consequences can lead you into interesting territory.

Evaluating a design, proposal, action or technique

Evaluating a design, proposal, action or technique requires you to form and present a judgment. This has to be a three-stage process. You must ask yourself:

1. What will be the outcomes of implementing the design (say), of putting it into practice?
2. What criteria should I use for evaluation purposes? (Whenever you see the word 'evaluation', think 'criteria'!)
3. How do I apply those criteria to the outcomes I have identified?

Let's take these one by one.

The outcomes of implementing the design. Essentially there are three possible methods that you can use: investigation, simulation and extrapolation.

Investigation involves actually putting the design or proposal into practice or trying out the action or technique, perhaps on a small scale, as a pilot study or trial run. Here, as when investigating a phenomenon, you go looking for both direct outcomes – the 'impact' of the action or technique, and indirect, consequential outcomes – 'repercussions'.

Simulation involves constructing a model in which a design or proposal can be tried out. This could be a mathematical model, a computerized model, a physical small-scale model – indeed, an analogue of any kind. Whichever you use, it has to be as representative – as lifelike – as possible. Once it is up and running, you examine it to see what the outcomes will be.

Extrapolation amounts to making an informed guess about the future on the basis of the past. So you might project current trends into the future, or extrapolate from past experience of implementing a similar design or proposal elsewhere: in another town, say, or under another political system.

If you are a physical scientist or engineer, you will be able to depend on your knowledge of the mechanisms that operate. If you are a social scientist, whichever of these three methods you use you will inevitably encounter the counterfactual problem both in imagining what will happen following implementation and in imagining what would happen if implementation did not take place – the do-nothing scenario – as you must do if you are taking the latter as your 'benchmark' for ascertaining effects. You will often also have to face up to the possibility that whatever 'effects' you identify may be the product not only of the design or whatever but also of other factors, and find ways of taking this into account.

What criteria to use? The criteria that you use to evaluate a design can be of two different kinds. They can be based on the designers' brief, e.g. the extent to which the objectives set out in the brief were met. So you have a question: To what extent are those objectives likely to be met? (Will it do the job? Will it sell?) Or the criteria can be 'independent' ones, such as efficiency and fairness, which you apply to the anticipated effects of the design. So you would ask: How efficient is the design likely to be when implemented? How fairly would the impact be distributed among the people affected by it?

Applying the criteria. The task you have here is to 'operationalize' your independent criteria, so you will be able to recognize and measure efficiency and fairness (say). In the latter case, that will almost certainly require you to distinguish different groups within the population, ascertain the likely costs and benefits that will fall to members of those groups, and then make your value judgments. These can only be based on your own feelings. For example, should the greatest benefit-to-cost ratio be experienced by those whose 'need' is greatest, or those who 'deserve' most, or those who will appreciate it most, or those who will be inspired to do more to help themselves? Should the needs of future generations take priority over the needs of present ones? Only you can decide. Note, however, that you are highly unlikely to be marked on your decision: it will be your working up to that point that will gain you marks.

Exploring and resolving an issue or problem

An issue, often formulated as a 'what should be done?' question, invariably precedes proposals and actions. Issues arise in many different fields, and the language you use and the approach you take will vary accordingly. For example, in engineering an issue will be treated as a 'problem', to which a 'solution' has to be found. In social/public policy, a 'way forward' has to be found for which support can be mobilized.

But across very different fields there are common factors. Here are questions that you can ask about them:

● What is the imperative to take action? Why is it that 'something must be done'? Sometimes a problem has been badly formulated, and the 'real' problem not understood. Sometimes it is more important to be seen to be doing something than actually to do it.

● What are the objectives that action is intended to achieve? How specific are they? You may find that stated objectives are unclear and/or that there is no agreement on them. To solve a problem yourself you must be clear about your objectives.

● What constraints are there (technological, financial, political, etc.) that limit the range of actions available? Could there be an interplay, perhaps leading to compromise, between objectives and constraints, with objectives being relaxed if constraints make it impossible to achieve them, and constraints being relaxed if a high priority is attached to achieving the objectives? Again, to solve a problem yourself you must be clear about the constraints that apply and whether constraints and/or objectives can be relaxed if necessary.

● What is the history of the issue? Issues invariably have a history, a background. Investments have already been made, positions taken up. There is an inevitable reluctance to write off investment and to retreat from a position.

- What is the context of the issue? Invariably issues are connected to other issues, and whatever decision is taken will have repercussions beyond that particular issue. It will affect how those other issues are handled and probably give rise to further issues, frequently unanticipated ones.

- Who are the 'stakeholders'? These may be technical people, managers, accountants, officials, politicians, and consumers, people 'on the receiving end'. Different stakeholders have their own special interests and are likely to perceive the issue differently.

- By what process can the issue be explored and resolved? This could be a purely technical, information-based 'rational' process, and/or an administrative process of going through a prescribed procedure, and/or a political process in which many stakeholders participate. Whichever is the case, and whatever your discipline, make every effort to list the steps involved in finding a (re)solution.

A project that involves exploring and resolving an issue allows you to gather information about all these aspects: perceptions of the need and scope for action, history and context, process and participants. You can use a wide variety of sources, notably documentary and people whom you can interview. You will find yourself collecting the pieces of a giant jigsaw puzzle and assembling them into the big picture. This is detective work *par excellence*. If you can do this systematically – step by step – it will be much easier to stand back and monitor your progress. You will need to do this if the puzzle is not to get out of hand, and you get so engrossed that you overrun your time allowance and leave yourself insufficient time to write up.

Making a critique of a creative work

Subjecting a creative work to a critique implies that you will be 'interrogating' it, taking a questioning, analytical approach to it. Your taught courses should equip you with the necessary conceptual framework and techniques for doing this, e.g. for 'deconstructing' it (or 'reading between the lines', as it used to be called). You may also be making explicit your emotional reactions to it, and analysing those too. As ever, be systematic in your approach, so (a) identify the steps in your working; (b) list the questions you are asking; and (c) if making the critique involves you in applying certain criteria, make these explicit.

Discussing a theme

A theme invites you to identify the literature relating to it, to read the relevant parts of that literature, and to form views on it. Later on, when writing up your work, you will present your views in your dissertation.

Here are some questions you should ask when tackling a theme:

● Does my theme have some intrinsic interest for me and for the readers of my dissertation? A theme that has intrinsic interest will help to keep you motivated and capture the attention of your readers. Disagreements (debates, challenges, controversies, contradictions and inconsistencies) provide more intrinsic interest than agreements do. Themes relating to changes over time (developments, evolution, innovation, continuities, discontinuities) have more intrinsic interest than themes relating to static conditions.

● Have I some inkling about the conclusions I might come to? Even sketchy, tentative ideas will help to give your work some direction and to prevent your dissertation from becoming merely a string of unconnected points.

● Is my theme a manageable one? If the bibliography you are constructing has reached one hundred or so publications and is still growing, then almost certainly your theme is too broad. Stop what you are doing, and find a way of narrowing it down.

● Have I mastered the language of the subject? Unless you are really, really fluent in the academic-speak to be found in the literature you are using, you will be floundering. You will find it very difficult to read critically: to pinpoint the sources of disagreements between writers, for example; or to discover how the conclusions that writers have come to were influenced by assumptions that they made at the outset, the particular data available to them, or their commitment to certain theories or beliefs.

Arguing a thesis

Arguing a thesis involves advocacy: putting forward a case and backing it up with evidence, opinions, etc. It is important here to distinguish between your project and your writing up. It is possible to carry out a project that is basically an investigation, and then to write it up as a piece of advocacy, but be aware that if you do this you are in effect switching horses (or at least mindsets) in mid-stream.

Alternatively, you could undertake both project and writing up with your mind fixed on the task of producing an argument. If you are being encouraged by your supervisor to do this, there are certain questions that you must – absolutely must! – ask:

- What am I expected to do about evidence which could potentially be used to undermine my argument? Can I ignore it, or do I have to consider it? Considering requires you to be impartial: arguing does not. If your mindset is one of considering evidence you are closer to investigating rather than arguing.

- What am I expected to do about counter-arguments that I come across? Am I expected to consider these? (Again, considering requires you to be impartial.) Or should I deal with them by way of including defences against them in my own argument? You can do this by making a point, citing the counter-argument, then demolishing the counter-argument. ('I am arguing X. It could be argued that X is erroneous because ... However, arguing this would be to ignore the fact that ...')

You should also ask, as you would with a theme:

- Does my thesis have some intrinsic interest both for me and for the readers of my dissertation? (Why should they care what you are arguing?) Like a theme, a thesis that has intrinsic interest will help to keep you motivated and capture the attention of your readers.

Once again, try to be as systematic as possible in your work. Create your argument as a logical progression, a sequence of steps. Make a list of these steps in advance. You will certainly revise this list as you go along, but it will be a constant help to you in the process.

Project: Materials

Materials and sources

Undertaking a dissertation project on your subject involves applying your brain to something. That something is 'materials' that relate to your subject. Materials are to be found in 'sources'. Broadly speaking, sources of materials fall into five categories:

- Academic literature: publications by academics and other scholars (the literature that you will already have been exploring).

- Professional literature: in particular articles published in monthly and weekly journals catering for practitioners in the relevant vocational fields.

- Formal publications, such as statutes (acts of parliament); law reports; the annual reports of government departments, other official bodies and non-governmental organizations; company reports and accounts; the published proceedings of parliament and parliamentary committees.

- Data sources, such as census reports and published statistics of economic activity, and reference handbooks in which formulae and physical constants, for example, can be looked up.

- 'Subject matter', such as literature which you are taking as your subject of study (e.g. books, plays and poems), ephemera such as newspaper and magazine articles, and manifestations in other – performance – media, such as film, theatre, music media, TV and radio.

Use your library

Follow the advice given on pages 27–28 for tracking down academic publications in your library and others. If your library doesn't carry much in the way of professional literature, formal publications, data sources or ephemera, it will be well worth making an effort to gain access to professional or specialist libraries that do carry these.

Use the internet

Make full use of search engines, such as Google and Google Scholar. Familiarize yourself with the instructions that will enable you to carry out advanced searches. And be creative in thinking of words to type in. If Google finds 100,000 references to the term you've typed in you clearly need to narrow it down by adding more specific words. For example, if you're interested in households in African countries, 'household Africa' will find you around 1,130,000 pages; 'household Africa census' will find you around 185,000; 'household Africa census definition' will find you 140,000; and 'household census definition Tanzania' will find you around 10,600 pages, of which the first tells you that in the Tanzania Agricultural Census 1995 '[the] selected statistical unit was the Agricultural Household, defined as any household operating at least 25 square meters of land or owning/keeping at least one cattle or five goats/sheep/pigs or fifty chickens/ducks/turkeys'.[2]

The web is also the place to go to for authentic information of other kinds. For example, if you want to know how the World Trade Organization is structured and what its formal decision-making processes are, do yourself a favour and make your first port of call not an academic textbook but the organization's website. Type 'world trade organization' into Google and you'll find the WTO's website at or close to the top of the list of pages.

Extract knowledge from materials

When you have your materials in front of you, it is really important that you don't just take them at face value, that you don't regard them as unassailable, cast-iron 'knowledge'. Instead, say to yourself: These are the materials available, but having read them, *what do I actually know*? In other words, having first extracted materials from publications, you now have the further task of extracting knowledge from those materials. In the right-hand column of Table 5 is shown what you can reasonably infer from materials of various kinds: their 'knowledge content'.

Table 5: The 'knowledge content' of materials

Materials	What you actually know
ACADEMIC LITERATURE	
● Case studies, research reports and other materials ('evidence') gained from empirical investigations. These usually include not only the findings of the studies but also inferences and interpretations made by their authors	● That decisions were made as to what data to collect and how to collect them, and that these decisions were based on someone's judgment and preconceptions. Inferences and interpretations will be similarly subjective. What you know is nothing more than that 'So-and-so reported ... and concluded ...'.
● Published theories and hypotheses typically aimed at 'explaining' or 'making sense of' observations, making predictions and/or unifying	● That these publications exist – their existence is a matter of public record – and that they are 'owned' by their authors, who may have strongly

Materials	What you actually know
theories already in existence; writings that qualify or elaborate existing theories and hypotheses	proprietorial feelings about them and a vested interest in getting them accepted by others. They are to be tested rather than accepted unquestioningly. Try them out to see if they are useful.
● Published thematic material, such as reviews, commentary, critiques and argument	● That these publications exist, that someone had an interest in getting his or her work published, that someone or some organization considered it worth publishing and had an interest in publishing it. Accord these publications the status of 'so-and-so's opinion' and 'contributions to the current debate', to be questioned rather than taken as 'the truth'. Treat them also as potential sources of insights and ideas.
● Materials advocating or justifying a course of action	● That these materials are likely to have been created and deployed in order to influence decisions in a way that would benefit the interests of the advocates (i.e. they would stand to gain from the outcome) and/or advance the values to which they subscribe. Accord them the status of 'political documents', and treat them not only as rationally worked-out solutions to problems but also as the products of interests. Look out for omissions – information left out, especially if it seems to have been left out deliberately – and try to identify the beneficiaries of these omissions.

Materials	What you actually know
PROFESSIONAL LITERATURE, especially articles published in professional journals	Published articles are usually based on first-hand experience, the 'grass-roots' experience of participant observers in the 'real world'. As such, they must be treated as subjective – 'users' often have a set of perceptions very different from those of designers or providers – but they may provide factual information that is valuable because it comes from the real world.
FORMAL PUBLICATIONS	All of these can be taken as phenomena in their own right: their wording and their status constitute attributes of which you have unambiguous evidence. As in the case of other phenomena, you can attempt to explain why they took the form they did, why they came about when they did, etc.
• Statutes (acts of parliament), secondary legislation, treaties, European legislation, law reports	• Students of law, public policy, international relations, etc. can take these as premises on which to base legal arguments or to develop solutions to legal problems.
• Annual reports of government departments, other official bodies and non-governmental organizations; company reports and accounts; the published proceedings of parliament and parliamentary committees	• You can regard all of these as public utterances, written (or spoken) with one or more particular audiences in mind. While some spoken utterances may be involuntary (they just pop out!), others are likely to be the product of drafting and redrafting, so treat them as the output from a decision-taking process. What they do not say – i.e. what they leave out – can be as significant as or more significant than what they do say. Consequently they offer scope for the detective work of reading between the lines.

Materials	What you actually know
DATA SOURCES, such as	
● Census reports, social surveys and published statistics of economic activity	● That someone or some organization has reported these data in this form, *not* that this was the actuality. Some events and activities may have failed to be reported, or may have been placed in the wrong category; figures and descriptions may have been exaggerated to serve the reporter's purpose or skewed by errors of observation. Census data, for example, are well known to suffer from errors arising from the failure to count some people.
● Reference handbooks in which formulae and physical constants, for example, can be looked up	● You can almost certainly treat these as givens (i.e. as factual). Don't forget to cite your sources.
'SUBJECT MATTER', such as	
● Non-academic literature which you are taking as your subject of study (e.g. books, plays and poems) and written ephemera such as articles and reports in newspapers and magazines	● That published editions of these works exist. There may exist different editions of such works, amendments may have been made to the author's work in the course of publication, and there may be uncertainty as to who the author was.
● Performances in or transmitted by media such as film, theatre, music, TV and radio	● You will usually know for certain that performances were held, but different participants, viewers and listeners may have very different perceptions of what took place.

Having reviewed the relevant materials, write yourself a note to clarify for yourself what you know at this stage. List each item separately, and be sure to include a full reference to the source of each item, to help you when you come to write your literature review and compile your list of references.

Project and dissertation: Time management and planning

Resources

One of the most crucial resources available to you is your time. Strictly speaking, time can't be managed: it flows on and on, at the rate of 24 hours a day, seven days a week. What you have to do is make best use of the time you have got.

It's important to make a realistic assessment of the amount of time that you'll be able to put in to your project and dissertation. There are 168 hours in a week. Take away the time you need for sleeping, eating and other elements of daily living, and see what you have left. Twelve hours a day, perhaps?

Now think about the other demands on your time. Will you have to work on your project and dissertation at the same time as you are following taught courses: attending lectures; preparing for seminars, classes or tutorials; writing essays; doing laboratory work or field work? These will be competing for your time. Most students find it very difficult to achieve a balance between these demands and the demands of a project and dissertation, because of their very different time scales. There's a kind of Gresham's law in operation: short-term deadlines drive out long-term ones. You find yourself giving priority to the assignment that you have to hand in next week over the one you have to hand in in a month or two's time. Then all of a sudden you find that your dissertation deadline is looming: panic stations!

Clearly 'rationing by deadline' is not a good strategy. You need a longer term view. You need to plan. Even if you have the summer vacation to give your dissertation work your undivided attention, you still need to plan.

Plan your work

Planning involves two things:

- Looking ahead, envisaging the tasks that you will be undertaking over the next few weeks or months, both in undertaking your project and in writing it up.
- Taking decisions: selecting a course of action and committing yourself to it.

You have two kinds of planning to do: planning your programme of work, on both project and dissertation, and planning the form – the outline, the structure – of your dissertation.

Bear in mind that it is virtually impossible to draw up a work programme when you start on a dissertation and not find yourself making changes to it as you learn more about your subject. Plans crystallize, dissolve, and then crystallize again. At one moment you can see clearly what you should do next, then that vision fades from view and you're saying to yourself: Hang on! Where am I going? To take a concrete example, you might start off with the intention of writing a dissertation on the question 'Why did Bismarck resign his post as Imperial Chancellor in 1890?' and end up writing it on 'How is it that historians can disagree so widely about the explanation of a particular event?'.

So what should you do? I suggest that you do need a plan, but it has to be flexible: it has to allow for unforeseen contingencies and for adaptation. As you learn more about your subject your objective may change, new opportunities may open up, the limitations of your resources may become apparent.

Here are some suggestions to do with planning your work:

- Construct a 'dissertation calendar' for yourself. It should show the dates and days of the week between now and your deadline, 'hand-in' day. It should also show all events that will make a demand on your time. Stick your calendar up on the wall. It's important that you keep one eye on your calendar all the time.

- Set yourself a 'comfort deadline'. Aim to complete your dissertation a week, or more, before your actual deadline. This will make it easier to accommodate unforeseen contingencies, especially setbacks. If you don't have any setbacks, and do actually meet your comfort deadline, it will allow you to put the dissertation to one side for two or three days and then come back to it and read it through with a fresh eye before handing it in: always a good thing to do.

- Make a 'to-do' list of the tasks that you will have to carry out, and estimate the time that each will take. For a study that entails field interviews, it might look something like that shown in Box 2.

Box 2

A typical 'to-do' list with time estimates

A Carry out internet search on subject of study: 1 day
B Draw up list of relevant books and articles on subject: 2 days
C Scan literature to identify researchable subjects: 5 days
D Produce initial shortlist of research questions: 4 days
E Develop alternative titles to show supervisor: 7 days
F Consult textbooks on survey research methods: 2 days
G Produce preliminary draft of questionnaire: 2 days
H Redraft questionnaire: 1 day
I Pilot questionnaire and revise if necessary: 7 days

J   Carry out 100 questionnaire-based interviews: 14 days
K   Transcribe quantitative data from interviews: 4 days
L   Collate qualitative data from interviews: 8 days
M   Analyse data, formulate findings and think about their significance: 7 days
N   Check findings against literature on subject: 3 days
O   Produce preliminary draft of literature review: 3 days
P   Produce preliminary draft of discussion chapter: 6 days
Q   Produce preliminary drafts of Introduction and Conclusions: 4 days
R   Produce complete first draft of dissertation: 5 days
S   Produce final version of dissertation: 5 days.

Add these times together. In the example above the total is 90 days – and that makes no allowance for a spare week at the end before handing in or for any time off. If you have only two months to work on your dissertation, and plan to undertake the activities one after the other, you're in trouble. What to do?

The first thing to do is to see (a) which activities offer scope for compressing; (b) which activities can be carried out in parallel with others; and (c) which ones can't be started until preceding ones have been completed. In this example, you might be able to carry out C, D and E simultaneously, in five days rather than the seven that you initially allocated. Activities F–N have to be carried out in series (consecutively), but you might feel that you can't afford seven days for activity I, and that its budget has to be reduced to three. Now you've reduced the 90 days to 75. At this point you might well feel that although it would be ideal to do 100 interviews, you simply haven't the time, and you will have to be content with 70. This will also reduce the time needed for K, L and M. You might also feel that you have to restrict the amount of qualitative data that you will collect and analyse. By this means you could bring J down to 10 days and the series K–L–M to 14. The 90 days are now down to 66.

Where can you make further savings? Some ingenuity is needed here. Consider making rough notes for your Introduction, Discussion and Conclusions sections from the very beginning. If you have these notes to help you, you might be able to reduce P, Q and R to four, three and four days respectively, saving a further four days. Your total requirement now is 62 days.

If your target is 60 days, you could achieve that by allowing only three days for S, producing your final version. You don't need me to tell you that this is cutting things rather fine. Your comfort zone has almost disappeared. Your options now, it seems to me, are to reduce your interviews to 50 or even 40, or – better – to START SOONER!

Doing for yourself an exercise like this will bring home to you the value of starting to think about and do preliminary work on your dissertation early. In my experience, students who do really well on their dissertation start thinking about it at least SIX MONTHS before hand-in date.

Produce your first outline

Now write another note to yourself. Draw up a tentative outline, version 01, for your dissertation as soon as you can. (An outline, or plan, consists of the headings and subheadings you will use.) Something simple like the sample shown in Table 6 will be sufficient at this stage.

Table 6: First attempt at dissertation outline

1. Introduction
   Why topic is an interesting one
   Central question (research question)
   Methodology
   Materials
   Outline of following chapters
2. Literature review
3. Work done
4. Findings
5. Discussion
6. Conclusions

Your first attempt at a dissertation outline is provisional. Soon you'll review it and find you want to flesh it out and modify it. Dissertation outlines *always* undergo change. It is helpful to have a draft outline from early in the process, but you could easily go through a dozen or more versions before arriving at the final one. As I say, this is normal: don't be discouraged if you find it happening to you. It shows that you are being flexible, and learning, not that you are producing a series of faulty outlines.

Part Three

The 'middle period'

Keeping everything under control

You can think of the 'middle period' of producing a dissertation as beginning when you've decided on your subject and approach and get down to serious work, and ending when you move into 'writing-up' mode.

The middle period can be a scary time. You can't yet see your dissertation taking shape, so you need to have faith that things will turn out all right. You may come across new things which demand to be read, and find you've lost days while you were reading them. You may find you've opened up several lines of enquiry, and your project is opening out, 'diverging' rather than 'converging'. If you're doing practical work, you may find you're getting results that you didn't expect and have to reorganize your thoughts to take them on board. Early on it may feel as though you've got plenty of time to do the work – then all of a sudden you realize that the deadline is uncomfortably close. At some point, you may find yourself thinking: Have I taken on too much? And, if you're anything like most other people in this situation, you are liable to find your emotions going up and down. All this can contribute to making you feel tense and pressurized. While a bit of pressure can generate adrenaline and energize you, too much pressure plus uncertainty will generate anxiety – probably not a state of mind in which you think clearly and do your best work.

In short, you need to take charge of events. Fortunately there are a number of practical things you can do. You can take on the role of 'managing' yourself, you can get going on your literature review, and you can keep your dissertation outline under review. These are the subjects of the next three sections of this book.

Project: Being your own manager

Being your own manager means monitoring your progress, looking ahead to your conclusions, and managing your thought processes. I deal with these in turn.

Monitor your progress

Check with your dissertation calendar every day or two to see whether you're on schedule, ahead of schedule, or slipping behind. It is of course especially important to know if you're slipping behind, so you can either take steps to catch up or adjust the calendar.

Be aware of what you're doing in the here-and-now, especially if you have come up against a problem. In that situation, it is very easy to get sidetracked into displacement activities, such as 'binge reading'. At such times, stop, take stock, and address the problem. It may be that you need to take a day off and do something restful and/or recreational. (The back of your mind will carry on working even when the front is occupied with an activity, so you will probably lose less time than you think.)

Notice too when you are trying to do too many things at once. If you have a sense of things getting out of control – diverging when they ought to be converging – you need to detach yourself from the day-to-day and take some decisions about your work programme: what to continue with and what to cut. Even if cutting means writing off some of the time and effort you have invested in your project, don't hesitate. There are times when you must be ruthless!

Look ahead to your conclusions

As soon as you enter the middle period, start looking ahead to the conclusions of your project. Doing this keeps your goal in front of you. It's OK to make tentative guesses as to what your conclusions might be. (I emphasize the 'tentative': you must be open to the possibility of arriving at different conclusions.) If you don't look ahead, you are in effect going on a journey without even the vaguest of maps. Remember that your conclusions can be of three kinds:

- Your conclusions about the subject. If you are starting off from a question, your conclusions must incorporate your answer(s) to the question.
- A critique of the literature informed by the work you have done.
- Your reflections on your methodology.

Ideally you will write something about each of these in the Discussion and/or Conclusions chapters of your dissertation. So start making notes on them now.

Manage your thought processes

Thinking is an inherently untidy process. Our thoughts go to and fro, ideas and questions pop into our heads, we turn the day's events over in our minds, we think laterally and we think about future possibilities. We digest what we have seen or heard or read, we try to make sense of apparent inconsistencies. Out of this messy process we have to produce a dissertation that is essentially linear, that takes the reader through a logical progression from Introduction to Conclusion. Quite a challenge! Here are some ideas on how to rise to it:

- If your head is always full of stuff, or if your mind 'races', write your thoughts down as they come to you. It will free up your brain. Likewise, when new questions occur to you and possible answers come into your mind, or when you come across some interesting reading, write a note to yourself about it. Writing things down will contribute hugely to clarifying your thoughts.

- Take every opportunity to talk to other people about your project and dissertation. They don't have to be experts in the subject, and sometimes it's better if they're not. The point is not so much to get feedback – although feedback may be useful – as to make yourself articulate your thoughts. You'll find that talking about your work clarifies your mind; and since the whole of your dissertation amounts to an articulation of your thoughts, the more practice you can get at doing this the better.

- If there's no one else around to talk to, feel free to talk to yourself. It's not a sign of madness, simply a way of slowing your mind down. Even if you're a fast talker, your talking speed will almost certainly be significantly slower than your thinking speed.

- Write notes to yourself as you go along on your methodology (e.g. on practical difficulties that have arisen in applying it), on materials that you are using (e.g. on the reliability of sources), on your findings and their significance, and so on. Some of these notes you will discard later, but others will be prototypes of the building blocks out of which you will construct your dissertation.

Dissertation: Creating your literature review

What goes in a literature review?

It is a standard requirement for dissertations that they should incorporate a literature review. What should go in yours?

As we saw earlier (page 26), 'literature' comes in a variety of forms. In addition to academic literature, there is professional literature; there are formal publications and data sources; and you may be taking certain literature as your 'subject matter'. In most subjects, it will be only the academic literature that your literature review needs to deal with. However, if there is a significant professional literature on your subject, you will need to cover this too.

A good literature review does not take the form of a mere list of your sources with an abstract or summary of each one. If your literature review is no more than such a list, it will give the examiners the (accurate) message that you have not 'got under the skin' of the literature, that you haven't digested it, that you haven't been able to read critically. It will be a poor literature review, and you will be fortunate if your dissertation earns a pass mark.

To write a good literature review, you must ask yourself: What am I reviewing the literature *for*? The answer you should get is twofold. You are reviewing the literature (a) to provide yourself with a 'platform' for your project; and (b) to provide yourself with material for the discussion chapter of your dissertation.

While working your way towards these goals, however, you must be aware of a 'trap' that lies in wait for you.

The literature review 'trap'

Many students, when they start writing their literature review, feel they have to summarize everything that has been written on their subject. So they collect a mass of books and photocopied articles, and then sit down to write a potted summary of it all. Faced with this mass of publications, their task turns into a nightmare. They don't know where to start, they don't know how to organize their material, and when they start writing they soon find they are in danger of their review taking up far too many of the words at their disposal. Instead of heading towards 10 to 15 per cent, it's heading towards 50 per cent.

What's happening here is that their 'literature review' is turning into a review of the whole subject. It's becoming a long essay in its own right; it's taking over their dissertation. This is not what should happen.

The literature review as a 'platform' for your project

I made the point above that one of your purposes in reviewing the literature will be to provide yourself with a 'platform' for your project. This implies asking yourself: What is there in the literature that is relevant to my project, that provides me with a starting point, something to build on? You need to pick out – highlight – elements of the literature that you are actually going to use or refer to later.

Here are some suggestions as to the platform that your literature review can supply for your project. (Broadly speaking, they follow the list of types of academic publication given in Table 3.)

- Questions, as found in Question-to-Answer publications. You could take these or similar questions, perhaps applied to different phenomena, as your research questions, and see if you come up with the same or different answers.

- Descriptions of phenomena, especially in case-study form, as might be found in Question-to-Answer publications and research reports. You could investigate different but similar phenomena, with a view to carrying out a comparative study. You could take note of the 'dimensions' of the phenomena that the writer used (i.e. the features that he or she chose to measure and report on) and use the same ones yourself, or you might feel that the writer overlooked some significant ones, in which case you could point this out (with your reasons) and go on to apply your preferred set of dimensions.

- A summary of the current debate on a topic. Here you could highlight differences between writers, and unresolved questions, and then go on to explore these.

- An overview of the theories and associated conceptual frameworks put forward by different writers. You could highlight similarities and differences, as a precursor to testing these in terms of their internal consistency and their consistency with observations that you make.

- A summary of a particular writer's argument, which you then go on to test or to subject to a critique.

- An overview of an issue, where you highlight different perceptions of the issue and different proposals as to what actions should be taken, before developing your own proposals.

- A list of different aspects of a theme: you can then go on to discuss, taking each aspect in turn, what there is in the literature on each, before offering your own contribution.

- A review of different methodologies, highlighting the salient features of each, before going on to apply one or more.

- Literature can also provide background to a study: a historical background, for example. Such literature, because it is background rather than central, merits only a brief summary in your literature review.

(It may be that you need to review several kinds of literature. No problem: you simply divide your literature review into the necessary number of sections.)

If your subject material actually *is* literature, or is the writings of great thinkers, you will be referring to it, quoting from it and analysing it later on in your dissertation. So there is no need to do so at length in your literature review. (Otherwise you'll be repeating yourself later on. Repetition uses up words, doesn't gain you any marks, and is liable to irritate the examiners.)

Use quotations appropriately

In addition to serving as a platform for your project, your literature review provides you with material for the Discussion chapter of your dissertation. It provides something for you to get your teeth into. It provides you with quotations.

Students who are compiling a literature review often find themselves quoting at length from their source when they start. Later on, when they are polishing up and editing their dissertation, they return to these quotations and attempt to trim them down. This may not be an easy task, especially under last-minute pressures. So it's worth doing what you can to avoid getting into this situation.

When you find a quotation that you want to use, please think about what its significance is and what you want to use it *for*. It's not enough to say 'According to X, ...' or 'X states ...'. The contribution made by a quotation may take one of a variety of forms, each requiring to be referred to in its appropriate way. In Table 7 – reproduced from *Write great essays!* – I have listed these forms and suggested the appropriate ways to refer to them, and also offered some questions that you can ask about them.

Table 7: Using quotations appropriately

Type of contribution	How to refer to it	Questions to ask about it
Fact	X found, discovered, revealed, ascertained, notes, points out that ...	Is this fact universally accepted, accurate (so far as you can tell)? Have other significant facts been ignored? How am I using this fact?
Perception	X describes, identifies, distinguishes, categorizes; as X sees it, ...	Does X have a particular standpoint which causes him/her to perceive things in this particular way? Are there alternative standpoints?
Figure of speech	X regards ... as; compares ... to; suggests that ... is like ...	Is this an appropriate metaphor or simile? How does it assist my understanding? Do I want to adopt it?
Definition	X defines ... to mean ...	Do other writers have different definitions, i.e. attribute different meanings to the same term?
Assumption	X assumes, postulates, hypothesizes, conjectures, takes it for granted that ...	Do other writers make this assumption? Is it valid, justified? Do I wish to share it? If I make different assumptions, would I come to different conclusions?
Proposition	X argues, asserts, contends, suggests, hypothesizes ... that if A, then B; X supports, is critical of, criticizes ...	How can I test the validity of this proposition, whether it 'fits the facts'?

Type of contribution	How to refer to it	Questions to ask about it
Opinion	According to X; X tells us, says, thinks, suggests, considers, comments, agrees that ... ; X disagrees with ... ; in X's opinion; it seems to X that ...	On what grounds (evidence) does X base his/her opinions? Do other people hold them? If not, why not? Do I agree with X?
Value judgment	To X, it should, ought ...; to X it is good, bad, beneficial, harmful that ...	Do other people share X's value judgments? Why should I pay attention to them?
Claim	X claims that ...; in X's professional judgment ...; to X, it surely, must be, is obvious that ...; it cannot be ...	What is the authority on which X bases his/her claim? Why shouldn't I challenge that claim and authority?
Question	X asks/questions whether ...	Are these questions relevant? Are there other questions that I ought to be asking?
Reasoning	X infers from this evidence that ... ; shows from his/her analysis that ... ; X demonstrates how ... ; concludes that ...	Is this reasoning sound? Could other conclusions be drawn from the same evidence?

You may come across a quotation that strikes you as highly significant but doesn't fit neatly under any of the headings in Table 7. In that case, just ask yourself this simple, all-purpose, knife-through-butter question: So what?

Quotations on their own are 'raw' material: you need to 'digest' them, especially if they use the technical language of the subject or are expressed in an authoritative voice. Digesting requires you first of all to paraphrase the quotation. 'To paraphrase' is defined in the Oxford Dictionary of English (second edition) as 'to express the meaning of [something written], using different words, especially to achieve greater clarity'. Greater clarity is precisely what you need. In effect, you have to translate the quotation into language that makes sense to you. (Don't merely substitute new words for some of the original ones, or change the order of words in a sentence: clarify!)

The second step in digesting is to 'engage' with the quotation, to 'internalize' it, so it is not only clearer to you but part of the thinking and reasoning that's going on in your own head. Asking the questions shown in the right-hand column of Table 7 will help you to do this. It is only when you have asked and answered such questions that you have comprehended a quotation's significance and can demonstrate that significance to your readers. To get to that point you must of course be fluent in the technical language of the quotation, not merely able to translate it with the aid of a dictionary.

If your review as you have drafted it contains lengthy extracts from the literature, almost certainly you haven't fully digested what you have read. Now or later, take a fresh look at those extracts and for each one ask 'So what?' and write down your answer. If your extracts consist largely of description, again, shorten them as much as you can. You earn marks for showing the examiners that you can appreciate significance, not for your ability to copy out quotations.

Three final points about using literature:

- First, your coverage of the literature should be as comprehensive as you can make it. Don't run the risk of examiners saying that you have omitted to read something significant. If preparing a comprehensive literature review would require you to read hundreds of items, then almost certainly your subject is too broad – you must narrow it down – and has been 'done to death' by writers before you, leaving little or no scope for you to say anything interesting about it.

- Second, some sources are more academically impressive than others when cited in a dissertation. So don't reproduce chunks of text from standard textbooks. Depending on the subject and your teachers' predilections, references to material appearing in up-market newspapers might be acceptable, more particularly factual records of recent events and the utterances of participants in them, and comment by reputable academics rather than columnists.

- Third, and crucially important, you really, really must cite all your sources, i.e. give references for them, so that a reader could look them up for himself or herself if they wished. I spell out the reasons for doing this later on in the section 'Conforming to good academic practice' on pages 106–17. You'll see that one of these reasons is to avoid laying yourself open to accusations of plagiarism. So you must be meticulous about recording details of every verbatim quotation (in quotation marks) that you include; of every piece of writing that you have paraphrased; and of writings, lectures etc. the content of which you have digested and drawn on.

I appreciate that it may not be the easiest thing to trace the source of everything that has come into your mind. Even experts on plagiarism find this difficult. The authors of one well-known report on the subject themselves acknowledge that their suggestions and recommendations arise from a range of sources, not all of which they have cited:

> Some ... are gleaned from the experience of colleagues or more experienced practitioners, from conversations with a wide range of people at conferences, and from consultations with student representatives ... Where appropriate, sources and research findings are cited but it has not always been possible to unearth the exact origin of ideas or to use publicly available sources.[3]

The fact that experts in detecting plagiarism don't always find it possible to unearth the exact origin of ideas they have used sits oddly with the frequently encountered injunction to students that *they* must do so. But do your best. Even if you are not wholly successful, the fact that you have made an effort will count in your favour.

Multidisciplinary subjects

If your subject is one that is dealt with in several discipline-based literatures ('household formation' comes up in demography, sociology, economics and social policy; 'diaspora nationalism' in anthropology and international relations) your literature review will have to draw together the particular contributions of these diverse literatures. How to do this? Here are some suggestions:

- Get clear in your mind what the phenomenon is that you are concerned with (human behaviour and utterances, events, situations or whatever) and what observations have been made of it. (In your reading, ignore opinion, commentary, punditry: ask yourself 'What do I actually *know*?')

If writers from different disciplines notice different features of the phenomenon, you already have something interesting to write about.

- Master the terminology used by writers from the different disciplines and the concepts, theories, assumptions etc. that are in their minds. Make yourself a 'dictionary' of terms, with your own translations and illustrations. Then work out how they all fit together, or not: how they complement or conflict with one another. Now identify the *questions* that writers from different disciplines ask, in their own languages, when they 'interrogate' phenomena. Now see what you get when you apply the whole multidisciplinary battery of questions. Don't forget to include in your dissertation's Discussion and Conclusions a note on the problems that you have encountered in carrying out a multidisciplinary study.

Save your critical appraisal for later

Don't forget that when you have completed your project you will be in a far better position to deliver a critical appraisal of the literature than you are in the 'middle period'. It follows that the logical place to do this is in your Discussion and Conclusions chapters, not in the literature review itself.

Dissertation: Developing your outline

As your work progresses through its middle period, you must keep the outline (plan) of your dissertation – the headings and subheadings – constantly under review, even while you are concentrating on your project. Reviewing your outline in the light of your project work will help to keep your thinking clear and focused. Often it will become apparent to you that you could improve your outline. Everyone finds their outline developing through the middle period of their work.

My first suggestion for a dissertation outline (see Table 6 on page 66) was very much an all-purpose one:

1. Introduction

   Why topic is an interesting one

   Central question

   Methodology

    Materials

    Outline of following chapters

2. Literature review

3. Work done

4. Findings

5. Discussion

6. Conclusions

As you review your outline, it will become more specialized and detailed. In Table 8 are shown six general examples. Does one of them suit you? You could start from that model and adapt it by inserting headings and sub-headings that are particular to your subject.

Table 8: Six general dissertation outlines

---

1. INVESTIGATIVE AND COMPARATIVE STUDY USING DESK RESEARCH

1. Introduction

    Background/context

    Research question

    Brief review of literature on the topic

    Structure of remainder of dissertation

2. Methodology

    Review of literature on methodology

    Features to be compared and method of comparing them

3. Materials

    List of materials and sources

4. Findings (observations)

5. Discussion (analysis)

    Synthesis of findings

    Significance of findings

    Critique of literature in light of findings

    Reflections on methodology and materials used

6. Conclusions

    Answer to research question, in brief

    Further implications of the study

---

2. INVESTIGATIVE AND COMPARATIVE STUDY USING FIELD WORK

1. Introduction

    Why subject is interesting

    Purpose of study (question to be answered)

    Conceptual framework (way(s) of looking at the subject)

    Structure of remainder of dissertation

2. Literature review

    Practical issues and debates

    Theoretical issues

    Published case study material (other people's field work)

    Literature on methodology

3. Case study 1

    Work done

    Findings

4. Case study 2

    Work done

    Findings

5. Discussion

    Overview of findings: similarities and differences

    Interpretation of findings

    Explanation of similarities and differences

    Reflections on methodology and theory

6. Conclusions

    How purpose of study has been met, in brief

    Need for further research, in brief

---

3. TESTING A THEORY

1. Introduction

    The place of the theory in current academic thinking

Purpose of study: why the theory needs to be tested

(Implied question: Is the theory valid?)

Brief outline of methodology

Structure of remainder of dissertation

2. Literature review

Review of publications describing the theory

Review of critiques of and commentary on the theory

Review of publications setting out alternative, complementary etc. theories

3. Your description of the theory

Foundations: origin, postulates, presumptions, etc.

Variables, causal relationships

What the theory predicts

4. Testing of the theory

Against evidence: do findings corroborate predictions?

In its own terms: internal consistency, validity of postulates, presumptions, etc.

Against other theories: consistency

5. Discussion

Inferences drawn from results of testing

Validity of theory (answer to question)

Usefulness of theory

How theory might be improved

6. Conclusions

Summary of discussion

---

4. EVALUATIVE STUDY

1. Introduction

Context of the study

Personal interest in the subject

What is to be evaluated (e.g. design, policy)

Purpose of evaluation

(Implied question: How good is the design?)

Methodology: criteria to be applied, and how they were chosen

Structure of remainder of dissertation

2. Overview of the literature

Subject material

Evaluation studies and methodology

3. Exploration

How design or policy would be implemented

Likely outcomes and repercussions

4. Evaluation

Results of applying criteria to likely outcomes etc.

5. Discussion

Significance of results

Objectivity/subjectivity problems encountered

Quality of design (answer to question), dependence on criteria used

Implications of findings for design and policy-making processes

Critique of current practices

Other lessons learned

6. Conclusions

How good the design, policy etc. is

Value of this study: implications for future designs, policies, etc.

Summing up

5: TREATMENT OF A THEME

1. Introduction: the theme

Historical background

Overview of the literature: current issues and debate

Aspects examined

Methodology and materials

Structure of remainder of dissertation

2. Aspect 1

The literature

Observations

Interpretation of observations

3. Aspect 2

> The literature

> Observations

> Interpretation of observations

4. Aspect 3

> The literature

> Observations

> Interpretation of observations

5. Discussion

> Synthesis of observations and interpretations

> Overview of aspects

> Implications for current issues and debate

6. Conclusions: summary of discussion

---

6. ARGUMENT

1. Introduction

> Background/context

> Thesis: what is being argued

> Rival theses: why this thesis is being argued

> How the thesis is being argued: structure of remainder of dissertation

2. The literature

> Academic literature

> Professional literature

3. Construction of thesis

> Underpinnings: axioms and presumptions

> Edifice: reasoning

> Pinnacle

4. Corroboration of thesis

> Relevant evidence: academic (theoretical and applied)

> Relevant evidence: professional (documented experiences)

5. Alternative theses: their defects

> Relevant evidence: academic (theoretical and applied)

Relevant evidence: professional (documented experiences)

6. Discussion

Why neutrality is not an option

Why my thesis is the best

7. Conclusions: restatement of thesis

You can start with the outline that is closest to what you need and then modify it to suit your particular needs. As a general rule, you should try to *elicit* – to *discover* – the structure that best suits your presentation, rather than *impose* a structure on it.

As you can see, all the outlines shown in Table 8 offer you a systematic and logical structure for your dissertation. In my experience, these models work well for dissertations and examiners appreciate them, not least because the list of contents and the final section of the Introduction provide 'signposts' that are straightforward and easy to follow. And for you as a writer, it provides a convenient way of transforming messy, untidy, jumping-about thinking into what necessarily has to be a linear presentation.

Note: If you feel – or are instructed – that you must say in your Introduction what your conclusion is, do this by ending your Introduction with a sentence beginning 'It will be shown/suggested that …'. This sentence can provide a neat ending to the paragraph outlining the structure of the remainder of your dissertation.

Part Four

The 'end-game'

The challenge to complete

As you enter the 'end-game' of your work, seeing your deadline looming up will concentrate your mind and get your adrenaline flowing. At this point it's worth making an effort to minimize uncertainty. Uncertainty adds to your anxiety and consequently increases the pressure on you. This is something you already have enough of.

Consequently you must *plan* what you are going to do in the time remaining. This means looking ahead: checking that you have enough time for the work you think you still need to do on your project and for writing up your dissertation; and eliminating the possibility of surprises that might cause you to have an agonizing rethink. In this part of the book, I outline the work you will have to do in the end-game stage. You can see from the section headings how the emphasis shifts from your project, as you complete your work on it, to your dissertation. I have subdivided work on your dissertation into a sequence of four stages: finalizing your outline and producing a first draft; improving your draft; ensuring that your dissertation conforms to good academic practice; and final editing of your dissertation. You should find it helpful to follow this sequence: to distinguish the different stages and take them in this order.

Project: Concluding your work

Set a realistic 'cut-off' date for your project work

In the end-game stage, you must set a 'cut-off' date for completing your project work. This cut-off date must be realistic, in two senses. First, it must be a realistic expectation that you will actually complete your project work by that date: taking account of your recent work rate, you must judge whether it is indeed feasible to achieve that. Second, the date must be a realistic one in that it will leave you enough time before your handing-in deadline to do a good job of writing up your dissertation. All too often, students set a cut-off date, and then over-run it. This is asking for trouble. The underlying problem may be that they don't know when to stop. Students in this position do often ask: How do I know when I've done enough? If you find yourself in this situation, ask a different question: Have I enough to say in my discussion and conclusions? Almost certainly your answer to this question will help you to see how you can wind up your project work speedily.

The fact is that whatever your project, and whatever stage you've reached, there is always more you could do. If you haven't yet got to your cut-off date, keep an eye open for 'diminishing returns', the situation in which adding a worthwhile point to your conclusions would require a disproportionate amount of work. You can always add a short paragraph on 'further research needed' to show that you have given some thought to how your work could usefully be extended.

The eleventh-hour rethink

For me to say that you should set yourself a cut-off date and stick to it is to offer you a counsel of perfection. Quite often the unexpected does happen, and students do find themselves having an eleventh-hour rethink. It may be because they have seen an opportunity to add something brilliant, and can't resist the temptation to incorporate it in their work. At the other extreme it may be because disaster has struck: for example, they discover that there's an important book or article on their subject that they haven't read, or that they made an assumption early on which now looks as though it's not valid, or that they forgot to take measurements of a variable which now looks as though it's a crucial one.

To avoid the necessity of an eleventh-hour rethink, do the following things before your cut-off date:

- Check your literature. Ask yourself: Is there anything I might have missed?
- Check that you are still happy with all the assumptions you made earlier.
- Check your early results.
- Go over the notes you have written for yourself. See if there's anything that you would want to change. Check your reasoning. Look for inconsistencies and loose ends. If you come across any leads you want to follow up, make sure that it would be profitable to do so. You can't afford to get diverted down any side tracks.

Dissertation: Producing your first draft and finalizing your outline

When you are producing your first full draft you will almost certainly find that you want to revise the outline that you are using. This is perfectly normal. It is only when you are actually drafting chapters and sections that you come to realize that the logical place for something is not where you originally put it; or that a chapter is either too long, and needs to be split in two, or too short, and needs to be incorporated into another. Consequently, expect to keep revising your outline while you are producing your first full draft (and possibly for some time after). In effect, you develop both your outline and your first full draft until they coincide. You need to have an outline in order to start producing your draft, but as your draft develops you will almost certainly want to modify your outline. Never attempt to force the draft to fit the outline that you had in mind before you started to produce your draft.

From 'writing as thinking' to 'writing as assembling'

At the point in time when you start work on the first draft of your dissertation, you should have a collection of notes that you have already made: the products of 'writing as thinking' while you have been getting on with your project.

Writing as thinking, when you're sorting your ideas out, is usually a messy business: untidy, disjointed, spontaneous, and sometimes repetitive, because you find yourself going over things again. This is why short notes are the best way of recording your thoughts. But a dissertation has to be more than a collection of short notes. It has to be 'linear' in form: chapter after chapter and paragraph after paragraph in a logical sequence that is easy for the reader to follow. Each chapter and each paragraph has only one before it and only one following it.

You must be aware, therefore, that in writing a dissertation you are not giving an account of your work, with all the false starts and twists and turns that it entailed, or even of your thoughts, which may exist in your mind as a network of connected points or as a constellation of unconnected ones. Rather, you are in the business of *presentation*: you have to assemble your dissertation to produce something that is as linear as possible for the reader to follow. So when you start drafting your dissertation you move away from 'writing as thinking' towards 'writing as assembling', although – of course – you don't stop thinking while you're assembling your dissertation!

Create a 'linear' presentation

Turning your collection of notes into a linear presentation presents you with a challenge. What models are there to follow? The most obvious example of a linear presentation is to be found in fiction writing, in the form of the story. Here events are not merely a sequence along a 'time line': they 'unfold', with each providing the context for the next. Readers read on, not just to find out what happens next, but with their minds informed by each event as they encounter it. In the realm of dissertations, the next best thing is the 'Question-to-Answer' format, in which you lead readers along a logical track. Outlines 1–4 shown in Table 8 are of this kind.

The problem that you are likely to face is that the sections of your dissertation simply do not conform to a linear pattern. Here are four instances:

- You want to write a section on your methodology, a section on your materials, and a section on applying your methodology to your materials. The only logical connection here is that your 'applying' section draws on both your 'methodology' and 'materials' sections. There is no logic that compels you to place 'methodology' before 'materials', or vice versa. So how do you hold your readers 'in suspense', as it were, after the first section, while you lead them through the second?

- You have a logical sequence of paragraphs, leading from one on to the next, each devoted to a single point. Then you decide that a paragraph in the middle of the sequence needs to have another paragraph tacked on, giving more detail, perhaps, or dealing with a point you've come across in the literature. In effect, that extra paragraph leads readers down a side track: how are you going to get back on to the main track?

- You are writing about a number of points 'in parallel', so to speak – a number of case studies, or several different attributes of a phenomenon, or the view from different disciplinary perspectives – and there is no logical reason for preferring any particular order. In this case, how are you going to go forward smoothly after dealing with the last one?

- You have a 'matrix' of things that you want to write. For example, you have been carrying out a comparative study of England, France and Germany, examining (let's say) social, political and economic conditions. Do you have a chapter on each of the three countries, and subdivide each chapter into sections on social, political and economic conditions? Or do you have a chapter each on social, political and economic conditions, and subdivide each chapter into sections on each country? And whichever you choose, how do you subsequently get back on to a single track?

The answer to all these questions lies in giving your readers 'signposts', so that they can grasp your structure at a glance. There are four concrete things you can do:

- Formulate your outline using subheadings in addition to main (chapter) headings. Sometimes it will be helpful to use sub-subheadings too.

In doing this you are giving your readers a detailed map, not a schematic one. The more detail, the easier it will be for readers to find their way around your dissertation. You can also group chapters together into parts if you think this would help readers.

- When formulating your outline, put the 'side tracks' under subheadings or sub-subheadings. Material under a subheading or sub-subheading doesn't have to lead on to material under the next main heading: readers won't expect it to, and won't be 'thrown' when it doesn't.

- To get back on the main track after you've worked your way through several parallel points or case studies, or after a matrix of writing, where you have used subheadings, add a synthesis, review or overview. So, for example, you might end up with a sequence of four subheadings: 'Case study 1', 'Case study 2', 'Case study 3' and 'Overview of case studies'. It will be immediately apparent to readers how you have organized your thoughts.

- Use the final section of your Introduction to tell readers how you have organized your dissertation. Although this may amount to little more than a summary of your outline – and thus of your contents page – it will help readers to find their way around and reassure them that you know what you're doing.

Your first draft

Your first draft need be little more than a stringing together of your notes. Certainly there will be gaps, overlaps, rough edges, discontinuities and inconsistencies. The value of your first draft is that it will reveal these to you. You can then go on to deal with them in the course of improving your draft.

It will also be well worth while, when you're working on your first draft, to keep thinking about what you are going to put in your Discussion and Conclusions. The clearer you can be about these, the surer you will be about where the dissertation is heading, and what you do and don't need to put in the earlier chapters. If you haven't yet finished your project work, doing this will also help you to be clearer about what you need to do to finish.

Dissertation: Improving your draft

Build on your first draft

Your first draft of your dissertation will be a patchy, rough-and-ready affair. Now it's time to start improving it. You don't need to begin at the beginning and work your way through to the end: you can work on sections in any order. It's quite common for sections to 'grow up' together. But you must bear in mind that what you are doing is *improving*, knocking your dissertation into shape: you are not yet at the stage of polishing, and you should definitely not attempt to polish your dissertation until you have been through the improving stage.

Synchronize and tidy up

An important part of improving your draft is 'synchronizing' the various chapters and sections. For example, your Introduction must be 'in sync' with your Conclusions. You cannot afford to have an answer in your Conclusions that does not match the question posed in your Introduction, and this may mean changing the question!

Similarly it is only when you have made progress with your Discussion that you will know which bits of the literature you have used are relevant to your presentation, and can tailor your literature review accordingly, deleting quotations etc. that you don't refer to later. It will be a waste of time to polish up and edit down your literature review until you know what you are going to say in your Discussion.

Tidying up means putting things in their proper place. So check that your chapters and sections are in the most logical order. If not, move them around until you find it. And gather together components that are alike. For example, when you read through your first draft you may find you've introduced new questions in your Discussion: bring them forward to join the questions in your Introduction.

Make your dissertation reader-friendly

The examiners who read your dissertation will certainly appreciate it if you have put some effort into making it reader-friendly. Here are some suggestions for achieving this:

- Know your reader. There may still be some academics around who want to see a continuous piece of prose that is not divided up into chapters and sections. Check whether your dissertation will be read by one of these. If so, you must humour them. Divide your draft into chapters and sections, but delete the headings from the final version. Leave an extra line or insert a few asterisks between the 'chapters'. You may need to incorporate the section headings (subheadings) into the first sentence of the 'section', using a form of words like 'Turning now to ...', 'With regard to ...', or 'Consideration must be given to ...'.

- Give your reader clear 'signposts'. Include a contents page, and include subheadings (section headings) as well as chapter headings. Be sure to end your Introduction with a paragraph saying how the remainder of the dissertation is organized. And begin each middle chapter with a sentence saying what you will do in that chapter.

● There is no right length for chapters, but they usually turn out to have a 'natural' length. As a rough guide I would expect your Introduction to comprise around 10 per cent of your total words and your Conclusions around 5 per cent. If you have six chapters in all, then the middle four would each comprise 15–25 per cent. If one of those middle chapters has more than 30 per cent, see if you can find a neat way of splitting it. Likewise, if one of the middle chapters has less than 10 per cent, see if you can combine it with another. For example, if there is very little that needs to be said about your methodology, have a section on it in your Introduction rather than giving it a chapter to itself.

● Use lists where they will provide clarity, but do not use them just for the sake of it. Bullet points are probably best avoided. They will impart a staccato quality to your work and this could jar with the reader.

● Use illustrations, diagrams and tables where appropriate, and insert them into the text. (Don't group them together at the end.) A relevant illustration or diagram can make a point clearly and save you a couple of hundred words. A table can present a mass of data in a very concise form. The reader will not go through it in detail, but will want to refer to it to see if the inferences you have drawn from it are justified.

● It may be permissible to put some factual material in appendices, at the end of the dissertation. Again, they will be there if the reader wants to refer to them. No substantive part of your dissertation should be relegated to an appendix.

● Do not, under any circumstances, introduce new material in your Conclusions. This will certainly lower an academic's opinion of your work.

● If you can, when you have a reasonably finished draft put it to one side and out of your conscious mind for two or three days, then print it out and read it. As you do so try to put yourself in the reader's shoes. Imagine that you are talking to your reader, and check that everything you are saying makes sense. You are very likely to find there are points you want to clarify.

Write good English

It is beyond the scope of this book (and its author) to teach you how to write well in English. There exist many style guides and manuals, both British and American, but these are best thought of as reference works. However, there are two books, both American but available in the UK, that you should find very helpful, whether English is your nth language or your first. I warmly recommend the fourth edition of Strunk and White, *The Elements of Style*.[4] It is a pithy little book, setting out rules and principles which will give you confidence if you are a newcomer to essay writing and dissertation writing. When you have read it, move on to Joseph M. Williams, *Style: Toward Clarity and Grace*.[5] The central objective of his book is 'to show how a writer quickly and efficiently transforms a rough first draft into a version crafted for the reader'. It does this brilliantly. Williams knows all about academic-speak and how to simplify it. It is a book to be read carefully from beginning to end rather than skimmed or dipped into.

Style

Here are some suggestions of my own about style:

- Don't write in a polemical, opinionated and/or emotion-laden style. Your writing should as far as possible be objective and dispassionate. An academic dissertation is not the place for you to display anger or contempt, or to apportion blame, or to be sarcastic or abusive. Nor is it the place for 'positive' emotions such as pleasure or congratulation.

- If your subject and approach call for you to make value judgments, save them for your Discussion. In your Discussion, first take your reasoning as far as you can without being judgmental. Only then should you apply your personal judgments. And when you do so, make it clear what criteria you are using, what the basis is for your judgments.

- Don't use expressions like 'I believe' and 'I think'. You do not get credit for your beliefs, and your thoughts need to be based on evidence, so cite that evidence and reason from it.

- Don't write in a chatty or journalistic style. ('Journalistic' tends to be used as a term of abuse among academics.) Try to use language in a rigorous and precise way. In the interests of user-friendliness, I have written this book using the informal language of spoken English as much as possible. You should not follow this example when writing your dissertation. It may lead you to be imprecise, and it may give an academic reader the impression that you are sloppy and non-rigorous in the way that you think.

- Don't try to write like a textbook or an authority on your subject. An academic may use expressions like 'We consider ...', 'In our judgment, ...', 'As so-and-so rightly says, ...', 'The evidence suggests ...'. (Evidence on its own suggests nothing whatever, of course. The accurate expression would be: 'In the light of this evidence I think ...'.) All these expressions carry the implication that he or she is an authority on the subject and not to be challenged. If you as a student use them, what you say and write may strike your teachers as pretentious and inappropriate.

- Don't use long, complicated sentences when you can use short ones. Your meaning will be clearer. And you know from your own experience of reading academic books and articles how infuriating it is when you have to translate complicated sentences into language that you can understand. It is not good practice to infuriate your readers.

- Don't use expressions like 'Many writers think ...'. The reader will immediately ask: 'Who are these writers?' So give their names and cite your sources.

- Your supervisor and his or her colleagues may have very definite views about style. If you are issued with a style guide, be sure to follow it. In particular, find out if it is acceptable for you to write in the first person. Can you say 'In this dissertation I shall show ...', 'I feel ...' and 'I conclude ...'? Or should you use impersonal forms, not using the word 'I' (or 'me'), such as 'This essay will show ...', 'The present writer feels ...' and 'One would conclude ...'?

Dissertation: Conforming to good academic practice

Cite your sources

Using other people's writings as sources and acknowledging their contribution by 'citing' the source – i.e. supplying a reference to it – is central to academic writing. It is good academic practice. It shows a proper concern on your part with the quality of the evidence you have used and with substantiating your conclusion. Citing your sources will enable the reader to check that you have used your sources appropriately and that your reasoning is sound, as well as doing justice to the original writer's moral claim to his or her 'intellectual property'. Citing your sources also protects you against possible accusations of plagiarism.

Using and citing sources involves providing three things:

- Within your text, an extract from the source (a word-for-word quotation or your own paraphrasing of a quotation) or a statement of your own derived from the source.
- Also within your text, an insert of some kind: a marker or 'cue' that directs the reader to a place where details of the source can be found.
- Details of the source.

Please note that there is no single right style of referencing. Ask your teachers if they have preferences as to which referencing style you should use, *and* either to supply you with a style guide or to refer you to one. In some fields (medicine, law) there are standard styles in the UK and USA and other English-speaking countries, but in others there are not. Some publishers and journals have their own distinctive house style, too. As a second best, ask your teachers to suggest a book or a journal whose style you can follow.

Incorporate extracts into your text correctly

Short extracts: If you are quoting directly (rather than paraphrasing), and the extract is not more than a certain length – this could be two lines, three lines, 30 words or 40 words: check with your referencing style guide – enclose it in quotation marks. Check with your style guide too to see whether these should be single or double quotation marks. If the extract already includes a word, phrase or sentence in quotation marks, the guide may tell you that these should be double if the 'outside' ones are single, or vice versa.

Longer extracts: If your extract is longer than two or three lines, indent it. Your referencing style guide may tell you whether it should be indented from both margins or only the left-hand one. Do not enclose an indented extract in quotation marks.

Shortened extracts: It is permissible to shorten an extract by taking out words, as long as you do not change the author's meaning. (Never remove the word 'not', for example!) The fact that words have been taken out is shown by the insertion of (usually) three dots (i.e. full stops, or periods). You can enclose words of your own in place of the author's so that the extract still reads grammatically, but take care not to change the author's meaning. Enclose your own words in square brackets [ ]. If, as a result of your short-ening, a word that was formerly inside a sentence now begins one, enclose the first letter of that word in square brackets. (Again, consult your referencing style guide: it may or may not require this.)

Paraphrasing: If you are paraphrasing someone else's work, it is important to make it clear that you are doing so: use some formula like 'to paraphrase X, ...'; 'X appears to be assuming/arguing/suggesting ...'; or 'in other words ...' (after an actual quotation).

The bewildering variety of referencing styles

There are, as far as I can see, four kinds of referencing style in general use. You can easily tell which is being used in a book or article that you're reading because they have different kinds of insert in the text. Look out for the following:

- Author and date, e.g. Smith (1980) or (Smith, 1980). Full details of Smith's 1980 publication are contained in a list at the end of the book, the chapter or the article. I refer to this as the **author/date** style.

- Author and page number, e.g. Jones (117) or (Jones 117). I refer to this as the **author/page** style.

- Superscript, e.g. [12] The superscript, or raised number, directs you to a footnote (at the foot of the page) or endnote (at the end of the book, chapter or article) with the same number. Full details of the publication are contained in the footnote or endnote. I refer to this as the **numbered-note** style. (The British Standards Institution describes it as the 'running notes' method.[6]) It is the style used in this book.

- Bracketed numbers, e.g. (12) Like the numbered-note style, the bracketed number directs you to a footnote (at the foot of the page) or endnote (at the end of the book, chapter or article) with the same number. The best-known version of this is the Vancouver style, but you'll also find it referred to as the 'numeric' style, so I refer to it as the **Vancouver-numeric** style. Unlike the numbered-note style, the same number (bracketed) may appear in more than one place in the text.

Choose the most suitable referencing style

If you have some choice when it comes to selecting a referencing style, which one should you choose? Here are some things you should know about the four main kinds:

The author/date style

Varieties: In the UK and Australia the most common version of the author/date style is that known as the Harvard style. In the USA the APA, ASA/ASR and CBE and AIP styles are versions of this style.[7] It is commonly used in the physical and life sciences and the social sciences.

Inserts in the text: In the text you place an insert giving the author(s) and date of publication. For example: 'Smith (1980) describes X as ...' or 'X has been described (Smith, 1980) as ...'. If Smith had two publications in 1980, they are differentiated by putting letters (a, b ...) after the year. So if you are referring to both at different places, your text with inserts would look something like: 'Smith (1980a) describes ...' and 'Smith (1980b) concludes ...'. You might also want, or be required, to include page numbers, so that the reader does not have to wade through Smith's book in its entirety to find your source. Then your text with inserts would look something like: 'Smith (1980a, p.13) describes ...' or 'Some writers have concluded (e.g. Smith, 1980b: 17–18) ...'. Your style guide should tell you whether or not you are required to prefix page numbers by p. or pp., and whether it should be '(Smith, 1980)' or '(Smith 1980)'.

Listing: For every different insert, you write a reference saying where the source can be found. At the end of your essay you attach a list of all the references, in alphabetical order of authors' surnames. This list might be headed 'Bibliography', 'List of references', or 'Works cited'. There are a number of ways in which entries in the list could be set out – different style manuals prescribe different ones – but they all have in common that they begin something like: 'Smith, T. (1980) ...'.

Usefulness: The author/date style is most useful where all your sources are books or journal articles with one or more designated authors. The insertion of dates in the text may be helpful, as Ritter points out, for following the progress of a debate.[8] This style also allows you to add or subtract references easily if you have occasion to amend your dissertation just before handing it in. It is less useful if you have to deal with 'messy' sources like newspaper articles and editorials, the publications of government bodies or other organizations where no author is credited, broadcasts on TV or radio, or websites. And it is of no use as a vehicle for 'parenthetical' comments – asides – that you don't want to place in the body of your essay.

The author/page style

Varieties: The main (if not the only) version of this style is the MLA style, codified by the Modern Language Association in the USA.

Inserts in the text: In the text you place an insert giving the author(s) and the number of the page or date of publication. For example: 'Jones (117) describes X as ...' or 'X has been described (Jones 117) as ...'. If you are referring to two different publications both authored by Jones, they are differentiated by including the title, which may be abbreviated.

Listing: At the end of your essay you attach a list of all the sources you have cited, in alphabetical order of authors' surnames. This list should be headed 'Works cited'.

Usefulness: The author/page style is most useful where all your sources are books or journal articles with one or more designated authors. If your source is an article in a bulky newspaper, citing the page is good practice since it will help the reader to track down the article. It can also work satisfactorily even if no author is credited, because you can cite the title instead. It is less good with websites and, like the author/date style, is of no use as a vehicle for 'parenthetical' comments – asides – that you don't want to place in the body of your essay.

The numbered-note style

Varieties: Numbered-note styles include the Chicago and Turabian styles well known in the USA. In Australia, the so-called Oxford style and Cambridge style are also of this kind. In the UK, you may find it referred to as the traditional footnote style or the endnote style, or – as by the British Standards Institution – the 'running notes' style. It is commonly used in the arts and humanities, some social and political science fields, and law.

Inserts in the text: At every point where you wish to supply a reference or a comment of some kind, you insert a superscript, a raised number. You start with [1], then [2], and so on, through the dissertation. Even if you are referring to a source that you have already referred to, you give it a new number. (So no superscript number appears twice.) Variants of this style place the foot-note number in round or square brackets.

Listing: For every superscript, you write a note giving the reference and/or making your comment. These notes may be placed at the foot of the page on which the superscript appears, in which case they are footnotes, or they may be placed at the end of the dissertation, in which case they are endnotes. The notes will be listed in numerical order to correspond with the super-scripts. The list of endnotes can appropriately be headed 'Notes and references'.

In addition to the list of notes and references, you may be asked by your teachers to provide a bibliography. Normally this would be a list of books and articles that you have used for 'background' reading: ask whether works listed in your notes should also be listed in your bibliography.

Usefulness: The great thing about the numbered-note style is that you can use it not only for references but for those parenthetical comments and asides that would interrupt the flow if you put them in the body of your text: a comment on the reliability of a source, or on some quirk that it exhibits; a reminder to the reader what certain abbreviations stand for; a signpost to another source where a different point of view can be found; and so on. It is also convenient to use when you are citing an original source which a 'secondary' source led you to: you can simply cite the original and then say 'cited by' the secondary source.

The numbered-note style can be cumbersome if you've inserted all your superscripts and then decide you want to add or subtract a reference, because this entails renumbering all the subsequent references. One way of getting round this is by using your word processor's automatic footnote/ endnote system. Another way is to type out each note within your text and enclose it within ## ... ##: when you've finalized the text you can find these one by one, remove each one from the text on to the clipboard and sub-stitute the relevant superscript, and then copy them from the clipboard in batches of ten or twelve into your 'notes and references' list.

The Vancouver-numeric style

Varieties: The Vancouver style emerged from a meeting of editors of general medical journals in Vancouver, Canada, in 1978 to establish guidelines for the format of manuscripts submitted to their journals. The group agreed a set of guidelines which was first published in 1979 and defines the

Vancouver style. The latest version, *Uniform Requirements for Manuscripts Submitted to Biomedical Journals*, is effectively the norm for biomedical journals. The numeric system described very briefly in *BS 5605:1990* is very similar.

Inserts in the text: At every point where you wish to supply a reference to a source you have used, you insert a number in brackets (parentheses). (*BS 5605:1990* offers the choice of using superscripts instead.) Similarly to numbered notes, you start with (1), then (2), and so on, through the dissertation. BUT when you refer to a source that you have previously referred to, you insert its *original* number (*unlike* the numbered-note style). So if you refer to source no. 3 seven times, say, the insert (3) will appear seven times in your text.

Listing: For every insert, you write a reference saying where the source can be found. Your list of references will go at the end of your dissertation, in numerical order to correspond with the inserts. The list can appropriately be headed 'References'.

Usefulness: Like the author/date style, the Vancouver-numeric style is most useful where all your sources are books or journal articles with one or more designated authors. The inserts are less distracting than authors, dates and page numbers. But if you have referred to different parts of the book in different places in your text it does not offer you an elegant method of citing the different page numbers: it is therefore most effective where your sources are relatively compact, like journal articles or self-contained chapters in a book.

The Vancouver-numeric style is more economical than the numbered-note style in that only one reference is needed for each source (and so you will have no occasion to use *ibid.*, *op. cit.* or *loc. cit.*). But it is less useful if you have to deal with 'messy' sources, and it is of no use as a vehicle for parenthetical comments.

List your sources correctly

If you are using the author/date (e.g. Harvard) or author/page style, your list will be arranged in alphabetical order of authors' (or first authors') surnames. For a single-author book, the layout will usually be as follows:

> Author's surname I Author's initials or first name I Year of publication I Title (usually in italics but may be underlined) I Number of edition if not the first I Place of publication (followed by a colon) I Publisher

If you are using the Vancouver-numeric style, your list will be arranged in the numerical order of your bracketed inserts. For a single-author book, the layout will be as follows:

> Author's surname I Author's initials or first name (but these can go before the surname if preferred) I Title (usually in Italics but may be underlined) I Number of edition if not the first I Place of publication (followed by a colon) I Publisher I Year of publication

As you can see, the main difference from the Harvard style is that the date of publication is placed at the end of the reference rather than directly after the author's name.

If you are using the numbered-note style, your list will be arranged in the numerical order of your superscripts. This style does offer you some choice in laying out your references. For a single-author book, here are three possibilities:

> Author's surname I Author's initials or first name I Title I Number of edition if not the first I Place of publication (followed by a colon) I Publisher I Year of publication I Page number(s)

> Author's initials or first name I Author's surname I Title I Number of edition if not the first I Place of publication (followed by a colon) I Publisher I Year of publication I Page number(s)

> Author's initials or first name I Author's surname I Year of publication (in brackets) I Title I Number of edition if not the first I Page number(s) I Place of publication (followed by a colon) I Publisher

If you are using the numbered-note style, you may find yourself referring to the same source a number of times. There are conventions that you can use to save yourself copying out the reference afresh each time: the *'ibid.'*, *'op. cit.'* and *'loc. cit.'* conventions. *ibid.* is an abbreviation of *ibidem*, a Latin word meaning 'in the same place'. *op. cit.* is an abbreviation of *opere citato*, a Latin phrase meaning 'in the work cited'. *loc. cit.* is an abbreviation of *loco citato*, Latin for 'in the place cited'. (As you can see, I'm adopting the convention here of putting words that are in a foreign language in italics.) You can use *ibid.* when a note refers to the same source as does the previous note, either the same page or a different one. You can use *op. cit.* to refer to a work previously cited in the same list. And you can use *loc. cit.* when you are referring to the same place in a work previously cited in the same list. For example:

18 P. Levin (1997) *Making Social Policy*, p. 30. Buckingham: Open University Press.

19 *Ibid.*, p. 65 [Same author and book as in previous note but different page]

20 *Ibid.* [Same author, same book and same page as in previous note]

21 J.G. March and H.A. Simon (1958) *Organizations*, pp. 140–1. New York: Wiley.

22 Levin, *op. cit.*, p. 222. [The work by Levin previously cited in this list, but a different page]

23 March and Simon, *loc. cit.* [The work by March and Simon previously cited in this list, and the same page]

If the use of Latin strikes you as too archaic for words, you can do something like this:

18 P. Levin (1997) *Making Social Policy*, p. 30. Buckingham: Open University Press.

19 Levin, note 18, p. 65 [Same author and book as in previous note but different page]

20 As note 19 [Same author, same book and same page as in previous note]

21 J.G. March and H.A. Simon (1958) *Organizations*, pp. 140–1. New York: Wiley.

22 Levin, note 18, p. 222. [The work by Levin previously cited in this list, but a different page]

23 As note 21 [The work by March and Simon previously cited in this list, and the same page]

There are actually British Standards that give recommendations for citing and referencing published materials,[9] and these can be applied to whichever style you're using, so they're available if you haven't been given any specific instructions about style.

Whichever referencing style you use, try to be 100 per cent accurate, complete, and consistent in your referencing. In particular, pay attention to spelling authors' names correctly. A spellchecker won't help you with these, and errors in spelling names will give a poor impression to the reader.

Avoid accusations of plagiarism

'Plagiarism' is a subject on which many academics these days are exceedingly twitchy. They report more and more cases of students presenting pieces of writing composed by other people as if these were their own work, i.e. without citing the actual source. In most reported cases this is manifestly cheating: acting with the intention to deceive. One example of this is submitting an essay which has been purchased from an 'essay bank'. Another example is the 'lifting' of quantities of writing from an unacknowledged source and making minor changes to the wording in what can only have been an attempt to disguise the original source.

Understandably, cheating is taken particularly seriously when the mark for the work submitted will count towards the student's degree result, because if it is not detected he or she may be awarded a better result than they have earned. And this, of course, is seen as detrimental to the public standing of the institution's degrees, as well as grossly unfair to all the conscientious, law-abiding students who have worked hard for their results.

But universities have reacted to this situation not by cracking down on cheating but by producing elaborate definitions of 'plagiarism' and detailed regulations, and by issuing stern warnings couched in highly emotive language: plagiarism is a 'crime', 'stealing', the 'theft' of the original writer's property.

Much of this is rubbish. To 'steal' in English law is to take another person's property without permission and with the intention to deprive the owner of it: clearly plagiarism does not deprive the original writer of the use of his or her words. And even if you do acknowledge a writer whose words you use, you are not expected to contact him or her to ask their permission. Furthermore, should the original writer seek redress, their remedy lies in the civil law, not the criminal law. I find it grotesque that universities should be promulgating inaccurate facts and fallacious reasoning.

Furthermore, the definitions and regulations are often highly confusing. There tends to be a common core – you mustn't pass off other people's work as your own, which is fair enough – but they all give rise to more questions. If you unintentionally don't cite a source, does that count as plagiarism? If you use a quotation and cite its source, but fail to put the quotation in quotation marks, are you plagiarizing? If you use two or three phrases that you dimly recollect from a lecture or seminar or some article you've read, without attributing them, are you plagiarizing? How close to an unattributed original does paraphrasing have to be for it to be plagiarism? And what counts as 'common knowledge', so you don't need to reference it?

To make matters even more complicated, the word 'plagiarism' is interpreted by different enforcers of the regulations to mean different things. Many academics would regard unintentional failure to cite a source, or failure to attribute a dimly recollected phrase or two, or paraphrasing of an unattributed original into which some work has evidently been put, or an error of judgment as to what can be treated as common knowledge, as poor academic practice rather than plagiarism.

The current confusion surrounding plagiarism creates a predicament for conscientious, hard-working, law-abiding students, and some have certainly been penalized for unwittingly breaking the university's rules on plagiarism, despite having no intention to cheat. So what should you do? The prime way of avoiding accusations of plagiarism is to conform to good academic practice. My emphasis throughout this book has been on this, both in carrying out your project and in writing it up. In particular, make sure you digest the literature you're using and follow the advice given in this section, and you should be perfectly safe.

Claim copyright for your own work

It is not unknown for academics to get ideas from their students and pass them off as their own. If your dissertation is genuinely your own work, and you have properly acknowledged material drawn from other sources, you are morally entitled to claim copyright for it. Indeed, if you have had to sign some kind of declaration that it is your own work, it follows that copyright belongs to you. To claim copyright, all you need do is add © Your Name 2005 (or whatever the year is) at the foot of the title page or at the end of the document. (In Microsoft Word, for © type [Ctrl] + [Alt] + [C].)

Resist temptation

To cheat and successfully conceal the fact takes hard work. You may as well devote that work to doing the job properly. Don't be tempted, even if you are up against a deadline, to buy a dissertation from an outfit advertising on the internet and submit it as your own work, or to copy material you've found in a book or on the net and pass that off as your own. This really is asking for trouble. It raises no subtle questions of what is meant by 'plagiarism': it is an absolutely clear-cut case of cheating. The existence today of highly developed software for detecting identical text makes it almost certain that you will be found out. It is almost impossible to avoid giving clues if you have used someone else's material word-for-word or in a close paraphrasing. Most academics love detective work, especially if they can feel righteous about it, and you are challenging them in their specialist field. Don't even try! And the consequences can be very unpleasant. You are likely to be severely penalized – possibly being refused a degree or expelled from the institution – and subjected to a great deal of public humiliation, involving being branded as dishonest and a cheat. So I definitely do not recommend this course of action.

Dissertation: Final editing

Final editing should involve no more than getting down to your word limit and giving the text a last check for clarity and style.

Get down to your word limit

Count up the words you've used (use your word-processor's 'word count' tool). Reread the regulations, and check that you know whether appendices, tables, footnotes, references, bibliography etc. have to be included within the word limit. If the regulations are silent about these, you cannot be penalized for not including them.

If you find you're over the limit, do the following:

- Look for repetition and cut it out as much as possible. Don't present data in a table and also give a verbal description of what is in the table: stick to giving your inferences from those data.

- See if there are any whole sections you can leave out. (There may be one or two that are interesting but won't earn you many marks: omit them.)

- Minimize description and direct quotations from the literature. These will earn you very few marks.

- Use short forms. Instead of 'It was found by Jones that ...', write 'Jones found that ...'

- Look carefully at phrases and sentences you have put in brackets (parentheses). You may be able to delete these without losing any meaning.

- See if you can remove any factual material from your text to a table or appendix, if it will thereby escape the word limit.

Check for clarity and style

In an ideal world, after completing your 'improved' draft, you will have a few days left before hand-in. Print out a copy, and leave it for a couple of days. (Take some exercise, catch up on your sleep, go to a movie.) Then read through your draft carefully, silently or out loud. Almost certainly you will find a few instances where you haven't made your meaning clear, or you haven't written in good English, or you've made a spelling mistake which your spellchecker hasn't picked up. Make the necessary corrections. Go back to the section 'Improving your draft', find the suggestions under 'Style' (pages 104–5), and make any further changes that you feel would be advisable. Make sure the title page conforms to requirements and looks attractive. Now print out the final version and bind it.

▼ ▼ ▼

That's it. Job done. Take pleasure in what you have achieved.

Box 3

Using a word processor

Computer crashes and loss of work will earn you commiseration and sympathy but nothing else. Here are some suggestions based on my own experience with Microsoft Word:

BACK UP YOUR WORK FREQUENTLY AND PUT YOUR BACK-UP COPY SOMEWHERE SAFE! This is absolutely crucial. If you're going to be paranoid about anything, be paranoid about losing your work. Save it on your university's server, email it to your mother, put it on a floppy disk and/or USB flash memory drive. If you're working on your own PC, you *must* put back-up copies elsewhere. Never leave a floppy disk in the PC when you've finished work.

AT THE START OF EVERY DAY THAT YOU WORK ON YOUR DISSERTATION, CREATE A FRESH COPY OF YOUR WORK AND BEGIN FROM THAT. Click on [File], [Save as ...] and then alter the file name from v21 to v22 or whatever. If you ever feel that you have gone down the wrong path, you'll be able to go back to an earlier version and start again.

SAVE YOUR WORK EVERY TIME YOU STOP TO THINK. Just click on [Ctrl] [S]. Get used to doing this automatically. As an added precaution, close the document every now and again – saving your work, of course – especially when you break for a snack or a meal.

MAKE YOUR WORK EASIER TO READ, BOTH ON SCREEN AND ON PAPER.

1. Experiment with different fonts and font sizes to find some that suit you, and with the 'zoom' feature (click on [View]) to make text larger on screen but not on paper.
2. Use a line spacing of 1.2. Click on [Format], [Paragraph], then select 'Multiple' in the 'Line spacing' box and 1.2 in the 'At' box.
3. Use the character spacing feature: Click on [Format], [Font], [Character spacing], then select 'Expanded' in the 'Spacing' box and '0.3 pt' in the 'By' box.
4. Lift your eyes off the screen at frequent intervals.

PRINT OUT A COPY OCCASIONALLY AND WORK ON THE PRINTED COPY RATHER THAN THE SCREEN VERSION.

Box 4

Queries, feedback, updates, web links

If you have any queries about producing a dissertation that this book hasn't covered, or any suggestions for improving the book, please log on to www.student-friendly-guides.com and send me an email. I'll be glad to answer any queries, and all suggestions for improvements will be very gratefully received. And don't forget to check out the website regularly for updates to this and other student-friendly guides, and for useful web links.

Notes and references

1. Peter Levin (1997) *Making Social Policy*. Open University Press. See Chapter 4, Approaches and methods.
2. http://www.fao.org/WAICENT/FAOINFO/ECONOMIC/ESS/census/wcares/ Tanzania_1995.pdf [Accessed 14 August 2004].
3. Jude Carroll and Jon Appleton (2001) *Plagiarism: A Good Practice Guide*, JISC, p.8 http://www.jisc.ac.uk/pub01/brookes.pdf, p.8. Accessed 9 October 2003. Carroll and Appleton do acknowledge 'the irony and possible conflict of this situation in a report on the citation of others' ideas'.
4. William Strunk Jr and E.B. White (2000) *The Elements of Style*, 4th edition. Longman Publishers.
5. Joseph M. Williams (1990) *Style: Toward Clarity and Grace*. University of Chicago Press.
6. British Standards Institution (1990), *BS 5605:1990 Recommendations for citing and referencing published material*, London: BSI, pp.3–4. See also British Standards Institution (1989), *BS 1629:1989 Recommendation for references to published materials*. (*BS 1629:1989* has been amended by BSI publication AMD 10180 published 15 November 1998, and *BS 5605:1990* has been amended by AMD 10182 published 15 December 1998.)
7. APA = American Psychological Association; ASA/ASR = American Sociological Association/American Sociological Review; CBE = Council of Biology Editors; AIP = American Institute of Physics.
8. R.M. Ritter (2002) *The Oxford Guide to Style*. Oxford University Press, p.505.
9. As note 6.

Acknowledgments

It gives me pleasure to thank each of the many students who have discussed their dissertation with me, and the many who have attended my workshops at LSE. Without their questions, challenges, ideas and openness I could never have written this book.

Dr Liz Barnett, director of the Teaching and Learning Centre, LSE, for giving me the opportunity to continue working with students despite passing my official age of retirement and for tolerating occasional eccentricities, and to all my colleagues in the Centre for their affectionate support.

George MacDonald Ross and Gillian Cleave, philosophers, for stimulating discussions, conducted in one case by email and in the other over the matrimonial dining table.

Student Friendly Guides

Sail through exams!

Peter Levin

A must for all students preparing for traditional exams!

This lively, short and to-the-point guide helps students prepare for exams in which they have two to three hours to answer a number of questions which they have not previously seen.

Written in a straightforward and supportive style, this guide:

- Enables students to take control of learning and revision
- Cuts through academic obfuscation
- Explains the language of exam questions

It provides a range of techniques and approaches which students can tailor to their own personal circumstances.

Practical, down to earth and on the side of the student, this invaluable resource helps all students to achieve their very best in exams.

Contents: The strange world of the university. READ THIS FIRST! – Introduction – Part One: Using past exam papers – Get hold of past exam papers – What to look for in past exam papers – Unfair questions – The guessing game: What topics will come up this year? – Part Two: Formulating model answers – What are examiners looking for? – Interpreting the question – Methodology – Materials – Drawing up a plan – An alternative approach: the 'question string' – Choose your introduction – Argument or chain of reasoning? – Writing exam answers: some more suggestions – Questions for examiners – Part Three: In the run-up to exam – Revising effectively – Memorizing – Make best use of your time – Getting in the right frame of mind for exams – Part Four: On the day of the exam – Be organized

112pp   0 335 21576 9   (Paperback)

Successful teamwork!

Peter Levin

This short, practical guide is for students who find themselves placed in groups and assigned a project to carry out.

* Allocating work appropriately
* Dealing with people who are taking a 'free-ride'
* Resolving disagreements
* Working constructively with people who they don't like very much.

The guide helps students to appreciate the tensions between the demands of the task, the needs of the team and individual's needs, and to understand why people behave as they do in a team situation. It provides reassurance when things get stressful, and helps students learn from the experience and make a success of their project.

Contents: Part One: Basics and Context – What do we mean by 'a team'? – The benefits of working in a team – Teamwork skills – Academic teamwork and the job market – Part Two: Getting Started – Get in your groups – Get to know one another – Formulate your ground rules – Check out your assignment and plan your work – Part Three: How are we Doing? – Progress on the project – Progress from 'group' to 'team' – Personal progress – Part Four: Perspectives on Team Behaviour – Tensions: the task, the team and the individual – Team roles – Management systems and team organization – Team development: forming, storming, norming, performing ... – The decision-making process – Negotiation – Cultural traits and differences – Individual traits: 'cats' and 'dogs' – Part Five: Teamwork Issues and Solutions – The task: getting the work done – Personal and inter-personal issues – Part Six: Benefiting from the Experience – Getting feedback – Reflection – Applying for jobs

136pp   0 335 21578 5 (Paperback)

Student Friendly Guides

Write great essays!

Peter Levin

What every student needs for university reading and writing!

- How can students find what they need from the long lists of recommended reading?
- What kind of notes should they take?
- What is the best way to structure an essay?
- How can plagiarism be avoided?

This lively, short, and to-the-point guide helps students to study and write effectively. Practical hints and suggestions which really work are coupled with insights into academic writing, critical reading and methods of presentation.

This guide builds confidence and changes study habits so students can get the grades they really deserve for the work they put in. No student should be without it!

Contents: The strange world of the university. READ THIS FIRST! – Introduction – Part One: Getting started – 'I'm a slow reader' – Three stages in academic learning – Coping with monster reading lists – Part Two: Reading purposes and strategies – What are you reading for? – Making notes and translating 'academic-speak' – 6 Exploratory reading: How to summarize a publication – Dedicated reading: How to make the material 'yours' – Part Three: Targeted reading – The principles behind targeted reading – How to identify key terms – How to scan a book – Part Four: Writing essays – Discovering what's wanted from you – How to clarify your topic – Thinking it through: a note on methodology – An all-purpose plan – Using quotations – The writing process – Part Five: Referencing systems – Using and citing sources – Which system to choose? – Recording details of your sources –Part Six: Plagiarism and collusion – The conscientious student's predicament – How academic learning forces you to plagiarize – Avoiding accusations of plagiarism – The politics of plagiarism

136pp   0 335 21577 7   (Paperback)